D1327607

# Palgrave Socio-Legal Studies

Series Editor
Dave Cowan
School of Law
University of Bristol
Bristol, UK

The Palgrave Socio-Legal Studies series is a developing series of monographs and textbooks featuring cutting edge work which, in the best tradition of socio-legal studies, reach out to a wide international audience.

More information about this series at
http://www.palgrave.com/gp/series/14679

Michael Adler

# Cruel, Inhuman or Degrading Treatment?

## Benefit Sanctions in the UK

palgrave
macmillan

Michael Adler
School of Social and Political Science
University of Edinburgh
Edinburgh, UK

Palgrave Socio-Legal Studies
ISBN 978-3-319-90355-2        ISBN 978-3-319-90356-9   (eBook)
https://doi.org/10.1007/978-3-319-90356-9

Library of Congress Control Number: 2018939715

© The Editor(s) (if applicable) and The Author(s) 2018
This work is subject to copyright. All rights are solely and exclusively licensed by the Publisher, whether the whole or part of the material is concerned, specifically the rights of translation, reprinting, reuse of illustrations, recitation, broadcasting, reproduction on microfilms or in any other physical way, and transmission or information storage and retrieval, electronic adaptation, computer software, or by similar or dissimilar methodology now known or hereafter developed.
The use of general descriptive names, registered names, trademarks, service marks, etc. in this publication does not imply, even in the absence of a specific statement, that such names are exempt from the relevant protective laws and regulations and therefore free for general use. The publisher, the authors, and the editors are safe to assume that the advice and information in this book are believed to be true and accurate at the date of publication. Neither the publisher nor the authors or the editors give a warranty, express or implied, with respect to the material contained herein or for any errors or omissions that may have been made. The publisher remains neutral with regard to jurisdictional claims in published maps and institutional affiliations.

Cover illustration: Pattern adapted from an Indian cotton print produced in the 19th century

Printed on acid-free paper

This Palgrave Pivot imprint is published by the registered company Springer International Publishing AG part of Springer Nature
The registered company address is: Gewerbestrasse 11, 6330 Cham, Switzerland

# CONTENTS

# ABBREVIATIONS

| | |
|---|---|
| AJTC | Administrative Justice and Tribunals Council |
| ALMP | Active Labour Market Policy |
| BI | Basic income |
| CESCR | Committee on Economic, Social and Cultural Rights |
| CTC | Child Tax Credit |
| DPTC | Disabled Person's Tax Credit |
| DRT | Dispute Resolution Team |
| DWP | Department for Work and Pensions |
| ECHR | European Convention on Human Rights |
| ECSR | European Committee on Social Rights |
| ECtHR | European Court of Human Rights |
| ESA | Employment and Support Allowance |
| ESC | European Social Charter |
| FOI | Freedom of Information |
| HMCTS | HM Courts and Tribunals Service |
| ICCPR | International Covenant on Civil and Political Rights |
| IS | Income Support |
| JSA | Job Seeker's Allowance |
| MR | Mandatory Reconsideration |
| NDLP | New Deal for Lone Parents |
| NRR | Net replacement rate |
| PCN | Penalty charge notice |
| PES | Public Employment Service |
| SA | Social Assistance |
| TCEA | Tribunals, Courts and Enforcement Act |
| TUC | Trades Union Congress |

| | |
|---|---|
| UA | Unemployment Assistance |
| UC | Universal Credit |
| UDHR | Universal Declaration of Human Rights |
| UI | Unemployment Insurance |
| UMI | Unconditional minimum income |
| WCA | Work Capability Assessment |
| WFI | Work-focused interview |
| WFTC | Working Families Tax Credit |
| WFHRA | Work-focused health-related assessment |
| WSOR | Written statement of reasons |
| WTC | Working Tax Credit |
| YTC | Youth Training Scheme |

# LIST OF FIGURES

# LIST OF TABLES

# CHAPTER 1

# Introduction

The phrase 'cruel, inhuman and degrading treatment or punishment' appears in Article 5 of the Universal Declaration of Human Rights (UDHR), which was adopted by the UN General Assembly in 1948, and in Article 7 of the International Covenant on Civil and Political Rights (ICCPR), which was adopted by the UN General Assembly in 1966.

In 1950, members of the newly-formed Council of Europe signed the European Convention on Human Rights (ECHR), an international treaty to protect human rights and fundamental freedoms in Europe. The UK was one of the first members of the Council of Europe to ratify the ECHR when it passed through Parliament in 1951 and it subsequently came into force in 1953. However, it was not until 1966 that the UK granted what is known as 'individual petition', i.e. the right to take a case alleging an infringement of ECHR rights to the European Court of Human Rights (ECtHR) in Strasbourg.

Article 3 of the ECHR outlaws torture but it goes further than that in also outlawing 'inhuman or degrading treatment or punishment' and it is generally accepted that this right is absolute, i.e. that it cannot be infringed under any circumstances. Due to the incorporation of the ECHR into UK law through the 1998 Human Rights Act, the phrase 'inhuman or degrading treatment or punishment' is now part of UK law and cases alleging infringement of any ECHR rights, including Article 3 rights, can now be heard in courts throughout the UK.

There are three points to note about Article 3:

© The Author(s) 2018
M. Adler, *Cruel, Inhuman or Degrading Treatment?*, Palgrave
Socio-Legal Studies, https://doi.org/10.1007/978-3-319-90356-9_1

- first, the prohibition applies to 'treatment' as well as to 'punishment', so Article 3 is much broader in its application than Article 8 of the US Constitution;
- second, unlike all the other rights enshrined in the ECHR, which are 'limited' or 'qualified', Article 3 is 'absolute'. This means that no treatment severe enough to meet the Article 3 threshold can ever be justified and that there are no circumstances, such as considerations of what might be in the 'public interest', in which an infringement of this right is acceptable;
- third, use of the conjunction 'or' in the phrase 'inhuman *or* degrading' implies a lower threshold, which covers *either* 'inhuman treatment *or* punishment' or 'degrading treatment or punishment,' than the phrase 'inhuman *and* degrading', which covers both terms, would have done.

In a case brought against Greece jointly by Denmark, Norway and Sweden and separately by the Netherlands alleging widespread breaches of the ECHR following the coup in April 1967,[1] the Commission found against the Greek Government. In its judgment, the Commission drew a distinction between the different parts of Article 3, describing 'torture' as an aggravated form of 'inhuman and degrading treatment'.[2] However, it did not attempt to define 'inhuman' or 'degrading' and, in its jurisprudence, the ECtHR has not considered the components of 'inhuman or degrading' separately but has considered the phrase as a single, conjoined entity. But, broadly speaking, it regards treatment or punishment as 'inhuman or degrading' if it is premeditated and applied for hours at a stretch, and if the pain and suffering go beyond the inevitable element of pain and suffering associated with legitimate treatment or punishment.

Jeremy Waldron takes a different approach.[3] He argues that each of the components of 'cruel, inhuman or degrading', which are the terms used in the title of this book, should be considered separately. He describes his approach as 'textualist' but distinguishes it from what he calls an 'originalist' approach. Originalists hold that the proper approach

---

[1]   European Commission on Human Rights (1969) 'The Greek Case', *Collection of Decisions of the European Commission on Human Rights*, CD 186.
[2]   See Kelly (2012: 36).
[3]   See Waldron (2008).

to understanding rights provisions in the US Constitution is to determine how members of the founding generation would have applied these terms two hundred or more years ago. As he points out, in no other jurisdiction in the world is this methodology deployed and nowhere else in the world is it taken seriously.[4] Waldron describes his preferred approach as an 'ordinary language approach' that focuses on the meaning of each of the words in question. He argues that terms like 'cruel', 'inhuman' and 'degrading' represent unspecified standards rather than unambiguous rules and that the challenge is to determine what they mean in different contexts. He also notes that this necessarily involves making value judgments.

Ronald Dworkin[5] argues that one should do this by trying, to the best of one's ability, to determine what each of the terms means. He suggests that we should ask ourselves 'as honestly as we can and in as objective a spirit as we can muster', certain quite specific evaluative questions, for example, 'what really is cruel?', 'what forms of treatment really are such that no human should reasonably be expected to endure them?', 'what really is inhuman?', 'what really is degrading or an outrage on human dignity?' He notes that any sensible person will recognise that, as with all objective inquiries, the best you can hope to get is the person's considered opinion, and that opinions will necessarily differ.

Rather than, as Dworkin suggests, everyone applying their own critical views of what counts as 'cruel', 'inhuman' or 'degrading', Jeremy Waldron thinks that a better way to understand these terms is to recognise that 'they purport to elicit some shared morality, some common shared values, some moral code that already exists and resonates among us.' He thinks that 'they appeal to what is supposed to be a more-or-less shared sense among us of how one person responds as a human to another human, of what humans can and should be expected to endure, of basic human dignity, and of what it is to respond appropriately to the elementary exigencies of human life', arguing that it is more satisfactory to view these terms in a social and collective light than to see them simply as invitations to make our own individual moral judgements. Dworkin's approach is that of the moral philosopher while Waldron's is more in tune with that of the sociologist and the socio-legal scholar, and this is the approach that will be adopted in this book.

---

4 Ibid.: 12.
5 Dworkin (1997).

The ECtHR has not, so far, been asked to determine whether bene-fit sanctions in the UK, or elsewhere, are in breach of Article 3 and con-stitute 'inhuman or degrading treatment or punishment', and no explicit attempt is made to do so in this book. Rather, against a set of shared understandings of what the three terms 'cruel', 'inhuman' and 'degrading' mean, the book attempts to give a critical account of the benefit sanctions regime in the UK and to determine whether it is acceptable as it stands, whether it is capable of being reformed or whether it needs to be replaced.

The origins of this book can be traced back to a lunchtime seminar in the Edinburgh University School of Law on 'Punishment and Welfare' in January 2015. My colleague Richard Sparks, who is Professor of Criminology at the University of Edinburgh, invited David Garland, who is now Professor of Law and Sociology at New York University but is also a part-time Professorial Fellow at the University of Edinburgh, and me to present papers. The subject was, of course, familiar territory for David Garland but I was put on the spot and had to come up with a suitable topic. My academic interests lie at the interface between public law and social policy and I have a long-standing interest in social secu-rity. A paper on benefit sanctions enabled me to tick several boxes and I thought that there would be some mileage in writing about this sub-ject. The paper generated a fair amount of interest and I was encouraged to develop it. An expanded version of the paper was published in the *Journal of Law and Society* in June 2016.[6] As I became more and more engrossed (some people might say obsessed) with the subject of bene-fit sanctions, I followed up the Edinburgh seminar paper with papers on different aspects of benefit sanctions for a range of audiences. I presented papers at the annual conference of the Law Society of Scotland held in Edinburgh; at the annual conference on 'European Social Security Law' at the Academy of European Law (ERA) in Trier, Germany; at a semi-nar in the Institute for Social Policy, Housing and Equalities Research (I-SPHERE) at Heriot-Watt University; for the Panel on 'Workfare and Labour Rights' at the Labour Law Research Network (LLRN) Conference, held at the University of Amsterdam; at the annual confer-ence of the Law and Society Association in Seattle; at the annual con-ference of the Socio-Legal Studies Association at the University of Lancaster; and at the Northern Conference of the Public Law Project in Manchester. I also wrote blogs for the United Kingdom Constitutional

[6]    Adler (2016).

Law Association (UKCLA), the United Kingdom Administrative Justice Institute (UKAJI) and the Welfare Conditionality Project.

At this point, I concluded that I had said everything I was able to say on benefit sanctions. However, I then met Dave Cowan, the Editor of Palgrave Macmillan's Socio-Legal Series, who invited me, not for the first time, to write something for his series. After some initial hesitation, I concluded that there might be some merit in bringing together the arguments I had developed in the series of papers I had written and attempting to produce a coherent account of benefit sanctions in the UK. The result is this book.

I would like to record my gratitude to Richard Sparks for acting as midwife to the enterprise, to David Garland, for his continuing support and encouragement, and to Dave Cowan, for not giving up on me when he had good reason to do so and for helping me out when he really didn't have to.

When I was a full-time academic, I always seemed to be over-committed and, as a result, developed the bad habit of finishing everything at the last moment. Lectures, conference papers, book reviews, articles and research reports were all completed just before the deadline. This approach enabled me to get by but at a cost because it did not leave me the time to get any feedback for what I wrote. Now that I have retired, I have tried to change my ways and have come to appreciate the advantages that feedback and a period for reflection can bring. I am incredibly grateful to four people, all of whom read the book in draft from beginning to end. The four people are my wife, Sue Fyvel, who is not an expert in the field but turned out to be a very astute critic and a very talented proof-reader; and three friends and colleagues: Robert Thomas, public lawyer and expert on administrative justice at the University of Manchester; David Garland, sociologist of crime and punishment at New York University; and David Webster, at the University of Glasgow, who knows everything there is to know about benefit sanctions in the UK. I am aware that the book is not the one any of them would have written and that the views expressed in it are mine not theirs, but it is so much better than it would have been without their help. They corrected numerous errors and omissions, questioned some of my more dubious claims, pointed out when more evidence was required, and were not backward in coming forward to give me advice, much—but not all— of which I accepted. They all deserve medals. So too does Dave Cowan. No-one could have wished for a better editor. I would also like to record my gratitude to three other people who answered my queries in their specialised areas of expertise: Katie Boyle (University of Roehampton) on social rights; Evelyn Brodkin (University of Chicago) on street-level bureaucracy and on welfare to work programmes; and Jackie Gulland (University of Edinburgh) on conditionality in health insurance. It should go without saying that, whatever shortcomings the book has are entirely my responsibility.

The book comprises twelve chapters dealing with the terms 'cruel', 'inhuman' and 'degrading' that are used as a benchmark for assessing benefit sanctions; benefit sanctions as a matter of public concern; the historical development of benefit sanctions in the UK; changes in the scope and severity of benefit sanctions; conditionality and the changing relationship between the citizen and the state; the impact and effectiveness of benefit sanctions; benefit sanctions and administrative justice; the role of law in protecting the right to a social minimum; a comparison of benefit sanctions with court fines; benefit sanctions and the rule of law; and what, if anything, can be done about benefit sanctions. Each chapter ends with a paragraph that attempts to highlight the most salient points in that chapter, and the book ends with a short conclusion in which benefit sanctions are assessed against the chosen benchmark.

Some readers may be surprised that the book does not include a comparison of benefit sanctions in the UK with benefit sanctions in other countries. After all, together with Lars Inge Terum, I recently carried out a study that compared benefit sanctions in the UK with benefit sanctions in other countries.[7] That study was based on data from two surveys of conditionality in unemployment benefit schemes that were carried out by the OECD in 2011 and 2014.[8] However, valid comparisons call for commensurate data and, in this case, the only available data sets were simply not sufficiently commensurable.

The data from the two OECD surveys refer to the strictness of the rules outlined in legislation or in regulations and therefore describe how the schemes ought to work rather than how they actually work on the ground. In other words, they describe 'law in the books' rather than 'law in action'. But, as Evelyn Brodkin has pointed out, 'what you see in terms of formal policy may not be what you get'.[9] In addition,

[7]  Adler and Terum (2018).

[8]  Langenbucher (2015) and Venn (2012).

[9]  Brodkin (2013: 4).

the data refer to the highest tier of unemployment benefit, even where more unemployed persons are in receipt of unemployment benefit from a lower-tier scheme. Thus, they refer to unemployment insurance (UI), where a UI scheme exists, rather than to unemployment assistance (UA) or social assistance (SA) for the unemployed, whatever roles such schemes play in providing support for the unemployed. For these two reasons, I have concluded that the results of comparisons based on this data, are not sufficiently robust to justify including them in the book.

## REFERENCES

Adler, M. (2016). The New Leviathan: Benefit Sanctions in the 21st Century. *Journal of Law and Society, 43*(2), 195–227.

Adler, M., & Terum, L. I. (2018). Austerity, Conditionality and Litigation in Six European Countries. In S. C. Matteucci & S. Halliday (Eds.), *Social Rights in an Age of Austerity: European Perspectives* (pp. 147–177). London: Routledge.

Brodkin, E. Z. (2013). Work and the Welfare State. In E. Z. Brodkin & G. Marston (Eds.), *Work and the Welfare State: The Politics and Management of Policy Change*. Washington, DC: Georgetown University Press; Copenhagen: DJØF.

Dworkin, R. M. (1997). *Freedom's Law: The Moral Reading of the American Constitution*. Cambridge, MA: Harvard University Press.

Kelly, T. (2012). *This Side of Silence*. Philadelphia, PA: University of Pennsylvania Press.

Langenbucher, K. (2015). *How Demanding Are Eligibility Criteria for Unemployment Benefits—Quantitative Indicators for OECD and EU Countries* (OECD Social, Employment and Migration Papers, No. 166).

Venn, D. (2012). *Eligibility Criteria or Unemployment Benefits—Quantitative Indicators for OECD and EU Countries* (OECD Social, Employment and Migration Papers, No. 131).

Waldron, J. (2008). *Cruel, Inhuman, and Degrading Treatment: The Words Themselves* (New York University Public Law and Legal Theory Working Papers, No. 98). Available at http://lsr.nellco.org/nyu_plltwp/98.

# CHAPTER 2

# Benefit Sanctions as a Matter of Public Concern

It is a central contention of this book that benefit sanctions ought to be a matter of greater public concern than they are. They are ineffective, in that many of those who are sanctioned do not enter employment, and they impose a great deal of suffering on those who are subject to them. They can last for periods of up to three years and are quite disproportionate to the mainly trivial offences that give rise to them. This book seeks to demonstrate that many, perhaps most, claimants are not culpable, that many, perhaps most, of their 'offences' are minor ones that should not be penalised to the extent that they currently are. It sets out to provide a comprehensive account of the origins and development of benefit sanctions, to determine their impact and effectiveness, and to assess their compatibility with administrative justice and the rule of law. It concludes by considering ways in which benefit sanctions could be reformed or replaced.

The book starts by asking why, since they are so ineffective and cause so much suffering, benefit sanctions in the UK are not a matter of greater public concern than is the case.

## Ken Loach 's Film *I Daniel Blake*

Although Ken Loach's film *I Daniel Blake* drew attention to the problem of benefit sanctions in the UK, they have not been given much attention in the press. This is, in some ways, surprising because the issues raised by the film have been around for some time. In fact, it could even

© The Author(s) 2018
M. Adler, *Cruel, Inhuman or Degrading Treatment?*, Palgrave
Socio-Legal Studies, https://doi.org/10.1007/978-3-319-90356-9_2

be argued that the scale of the problems revealed in the film was on the decline when the film was released in October 2016.

The central scenario depicted by the film is that, although Daniel, a carpenter from Newcastle, has had a heart attack and lost his job, and been told by his doctors not to work, he did not qualify for Employment and Support Allowance (ESA), the main benefit for sick and disabled people who are deemed to be unable to work. All applicants for ESA are required to take the Work Capability Assessment (WCA) test. This comprises a set of 17 descriptors covering physical and mental capacity for work such as walking, lifting, concentrating and not getting angry, and applicants are given a score depending on how well (or how badly) they do. A total of 15 points is needed to qualify for benefit.

In the film Daniel fails to get 15 points and receives a letter from the Department for Work and Pensions (DWP) telling him that he has failed the test and is therefore fit for work. He phones the DWP, which administers ESA, saying that he wants to appeal, but is told that he must first request a Mandatory Reconsideration (MR) and that he cannot do so until he has had a phone call from the DWP decision-maker.

In the past, claimants could appeal directly to a tribunal if their application for benefit was turned down but, in 2012, in order to reduce the tribunal caseload and the costs of appealing, the DWP decided that they had to go through MR, which is carried out by officials, first. While appellants are awaiting the outcome, they do not receive any money.

The film depicts the Catch 22 situation facing many claimants who wish to challenge their ESA decisions. The only way for them to get some money is to apply for Job Seeker's Allowance (JSA), the main benefit (at the time) for unemployed people who are deemed to be able to work. But, if they wished to claim JSA, they would have to declare that they were fit for work, despite arguing that they were not.

Some of the other scenarios in the film refer to situations that are regularly encountered in the UK. They include the following:

- The DWP wants to conduct all its business online, although many people are not able to, or comfortable about, doing so. Job Centres do not appear to accept any obligation to ensure that help is provided for those who need it. Although those in receipt of benefit may be sent on computing courses, Job Centre staff never seem to sit down with claimants to take them through the application process.

- Because housing is so expensive in London, local authorities, which have a legal duty to provide housing for homeless people, are increasingly housing them in parts of the UK where housing is cheaper. This is how Katie, who meets Daniel in the Job Centre, ends up in the north of England.
- Benefit sanctions, i.e. suspensions of benefit for periods ranging from four weeks to three years, for failing to meet the conditions of entitlement to benefit, had reached almost epidemic proportions in the period between 2010 and 2014, when the idea for the film was being developed. In 2012 and 2013, more people received a benefit sanction than received a fine in the criminal courts. Thus, Katie, a struggling single mother with two children, who is befriended by Daniel, was sanctioned for turning up 10 minutes late for an appointment. Her experiences illustrate Ken Loach's contention that claiming benefits in the UK is 'a Kafkaesque situation [which is] designed to frustrate and humiliate the claimant to such an extent that they drop out of the system and stop pursuing their right to ask for support if necessary'.[1]
- Those who are sanctioned can, after an interval of time, apply for a hardship payment (paid at 60% of the benefit rate). 'Vulnerable' claimants used to be paid at 80% of the benefit rate but this is no longer the case under Universal Credit (UC), to which recipients of income-based JSA and ESA are being transferred. Claimants may, as happened in the case of Katie in *I Daniel Blake*, be offered vouchers for a food bank to help them cope with being sanctioned. Food banks distribute food products donated by members of the public, supermarkets and local authorities as a 'last resort' to those who would otherwise go hungry. And this is what drove Katie into prostitution.

The powerful appeal of the film was largely based on showing that Daniel Blake was deserving of help and mistreated by the state and one of the aims of this book is to show that this is the case with many, perhaps most, claimants who are sanctioned.

The film is undoubtedly bleak, but it is, at the same time, very realistic. It does, admittedly, describe a 'worst case scenario'—very few

---

[1] Jones (2016).

people die before their appeal is heard—but the benefit system is unduly harsh and insensitive, and many claimants undoubtedly experience unnecessary suffering. The amount of begging on the streets in the UK, often by people who have run up against the social security system, provides visible evidence of that.

## THE PUBLIC'S RESPONSE TO BENEFIT SANCTIONS

50 years before the release of *I Daniel Blake*, on 16 November 1966, the BBC broadcast *Cathy Come Home*, a film that was also directed by Ken Loach. This film was about homelessness and alerted the public, the media, and the government to the scale of the housing crisis. It is estimated that, on its first broadcast, the film was watched by 12 million people and it led to a public outcry and calls for action after its transmission. It also led to a huge surge of support for Shelter, the campaigning organisation that was launched on 1 December 1966. Shelter, which evolved out of the work on behalf of homeless people that had been carried out in Notting Hill in West London, quickly grew into a national organisation and gained many new supporters. Eight years later, largely due to the efforts of Shelter, the Callaghan Government[2] introduced a piece of landmark legislation, the Housing (Homeless Persons) Act 1977, which, for the first time, put forward a statutory definition of homelessness, gave rights to the homeless and placed a statutory duty on local housing authorities to ensure that advice and assistance to households who are homeless or threatened with homelessness were available free of charge.[3]

Although it is probably too early to say whether *I Daniel Blake* will have the same or a comparable impact, the signs, at the time of writing some 18 months after it was awarded the Palme d'Or at Cannes, are not auspicious. Is this because, in the case of benefit sanctions in the UK today, the thinking that lies behind them and the way they are implemented does not constitute as serious a case of injustice as homelessness did 50 years ago? Or is it because those who are subject to sanctions are not seen as being as deserving of public sympathy and concern as those who are homeless?

---

[2] James Callaghan succeeded Harold Wilson as Labour Prime Minister in March 1976.
[3] See Crowson (2012).

The unemployed and the homeless do have some characteristics in common, not least the fact that they are frequently blamed for the circumstances in which they find themselves.[4] Those who are subject to benefit sanctions may be blamed for being unemployed in the first place and subsequently for not doing what is expected of them, just as those who are homeless may be blamed for not having anywhere to live. However, there is a good deal of evidence that public attitudes towards those who are subject to benefit sanctions, i.e. those who are unemployed and in receipt of benefit, are even more negative than public attitudes towards the homeless. Thus, in the case of benefit sanctions, people may be more likely to think of those who are sanctioned as undeserving and that sanctions are an appropriate response to rule breaking. This would suggest that those who are sanctioned are often thought of in the same way as offenders, for whom there is also little sympathy. On the other hand, in the case of homelessness, those who have nowhere to stay are thought of as victims of unscrupulous landlords. In addition, whereas Shelter was, and continues to be, very effective in drawing attention to the problem of homelessness, no comparable organisation has set out to draw attention to the problems faced by those who are subject to benefit sanctions. These arguments go a long way towards explaining why *I Daniel Blake* did not strike the same chord with the public as *Cathy Come Home* undoubtedly did.

In 2011, several years before *I Daniel Blake* was written, made and released, *YouGov*, a very well-respected, internet-based market research and data analysis firm, carried out a poll to investigate public perceptions of fairness, poverty and benefits. 50% of the weighted sample of 2407 respondents thought that out-of-work benefits were too high, and discouraged people from finding work, 70% thought that people on Jobseekers Allowance who refused work or failed to attend interviews should lose half or more of their benefits. Responses to the question 'What sanctions, if any should people claiming JSA who refuse job offers or interviews or who do not comply with their Jobseeker's Agreement be given?' are set out in Table 2.1.

When respondents were asked whether this should apply to people in various family circumstances, they were more sympathetic to people with dependent children, with most respondents thinking they should lose at most a small proportion of their benefits; and to carers, with a majority

---

4  The classic treatment of this process is Ryan (1971).

**Table 2.1**   Public attitudes to benefit sanctions

|  | *If they refuse job offers or fail to attend interviews* | *If they do not comply with jobseeker's agreement* |
|---|---|---|
| Should not lose any of their benefits | 6 | 7 |
| Should lose a small amount of their benefits (say 10%) | 19 | 18 |
| Should lose a large amount of their benefits but keep enough to cover their basic needs | 49 | 47 |
| Should lose all their benefits, regardless of what hardship it causes | 21 | 21 |
| Don't know | 8 | 6 |

*Source* YouGov Fairness Poll, April 2011, available at http://ukpollingreport.co.uk/blog/archives/date/2011/04

saying that they should not face any sanctions at all. 80% of respondents agreed with the suggestion that people who have been out of work for 12 months should be required to do community work in return for their benefits.

## BENEFIT CLAIMANTS AS A MATTER OF PUBLIC DISAPPROVAL

The generally positive response of the critics to *I Daniel Blake* can be contrasted not only with the rather hawkish attitudes to benefit sanctions revealed in the *YouGov* survey but also with the generally negative attitudes of the public towards benefit claimants. Since 1987, the *British Social Attitudes Survey* has asked a representative sample of the population a series of questions about public attitudes to the unemployed and to the benefits system. In 2014, the BSA published a report that analysed survey responses to three questions: are benefits enough to live on; are benefit claimants deserving of help; and should spending on benefits be reduced or raised? The responses to each of these questions will be considered in turn.

### *Are Benefits Enough to Live On?*

Respondents were asked to assess the living standards of a 25-year-old unemployed single woman on benefits, first with no further information

**Table 2.2**  Perceived standards of living of unemployed single person living alone on benefits, 1994–2013

| | Before being told the true amount of benefit | | | After being told the true amount of benefit | | |
|---|---|---|---|---|---|---|
| | 1994 | 2000 | 2013 | 1994 | 2000 | 2013 |
| *Unemployed person* ... | | | | | | |
| Has more than enough | 1% | 2% | 7% | 2% | 3% | 4% |
| Has enough | 21% | 21% | 37% | 25% | 28% | 36% |
| Is hard up | 54% | 46% | 36% | 55% | 55% | 46% |
| Is really poor | 10% | 10% | 6% | 16% | 13% | 10% |
| *Combined answers* | | | | | | |
| Enough or more | 22% | 34% | 44% | 27% | 31% | 42% |
| Not enough | 70% | 56% | 44% | 71% | 68% | 56% |
| Unweighted base | 1167 | 3426 | 3244 | 1167 | 3426 | 3244 |

*Source* Baumberg (2014: Table 6.1)

and then after being told how much benefit she received. The results are set out in Table 2.2.

In 2013, opinion was divided on whether she would have enough to live on but, when told how much benefit she actually received, a majority (56%) thought she would not have enough. Nevertheless, public perceptions of unemployment benefit levels have clearly hardened over the last 20 years with more respondents saying that she would have enough to live on (up 22% before being told how much benefit she received) and fewer saying that they would not (down 26%).

### Are Benefit Claimants Deserving of Help?

Respondents were also asked whether they believed that (i) large numbers of claimants falsely claim benefit; (ii) benefits discourage work; (iii) most unemployed claimants could find work; and (iv) many unemployed claimants do not deserve to be helped. Time-series data, set out in Fig. 2.1, make it clear that attitudes have changed quite considerably over the past two decades and that, in 2013, claimants were viewed as less deserving than they were 20 years previously and this was particularly true for attitudes towards unemployed claimants.

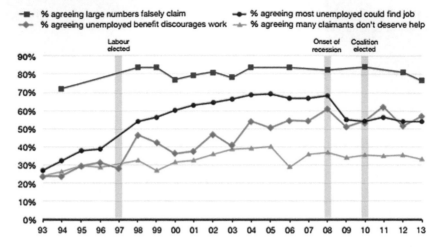

**Fig. 2.1** Trends in perceived deservingness of benefit claimants, 1993–2013 (*Source* Baumberg 2014: Fig. 6.1)

The data indicate that attitudes towards unemployed claimants softened in the latter years of the Labour Government as the economic recession hit in 2008/2009, although levels of support for claimants did not return to what they had been 20 years previously.

The extent of support for the claim that many social security claimants do not deserve help rose from 24% in 1993 to 31% in 2000, and to 40% in 2005, before falling back to 33% in 2013. Although support for the claim that unemployment benefits discourage work have fluctuated over the 20-year period, the underlying trend has been upwards from 24% in 1993 to 46% in 1998 and 57% in 2013.

Support for the claim that most unemployed people could find a job if they wanted one increased very markedly from 27% in 1993 to 69% in 2005, remaining at that level until 2008 and then falling back somewhat to 54% in 2013. Views on whether large numbers of claimants fiddle the system in one way or another were very high indeed but have been rather stable and have fluctuated between 72 and 82% over the 20-year period. They fell slightly from 82% in 2010 to 77% in 2013.

The findings reported above are important because, if the public have been led to believe that fiddling is extensive, then using sanctions may seem justified. In fact, the extent of fraud is much less than many people think.

A poll conducted by the Trades Union Congress (TUC) in 2012 found that perceptions among the British public were that benefit fraud was high—on average people thought that 27% of the British social security budget was claimed fraudulently. However, official UK Government figures have stated that the proportion of fraud stood at 0.7% of the total social security budget in 2011/2012.[5]

The time-series data described above indicate that, in 2013, over half (54%) of the British public agreed that 'most unemployed people could find a job if they really wanted one' and a similar proportion (57%) agreed that 'unemployment benefits are too high and discourage people from finding paid work'. Beyond unemployment benefits, three-quarters (77%) of people agreed that 'large numbers of people' falsely claim benefits. However, only a minority (33%) agreed that 'most people on the dole are fiddling in one way or another' or that 'many people who get social security do not really deserve any help'. According to Baumberg,[6] the most likely explanation for this apparent difference is that most people (77%) think that 'large numbers ... falsely claim benefits'. But by 'large numbers', they mean (on average) a large minority, not a majority. Hence only minorities in 2013 agreed that 'many people who get social security do not really deserve any help', or that 'most people on the dole are fiddling' (both 33%). This fits with other evidence that people are very concerned about some undeserving claimants getting benefits, but do not think that most claimants are outright false or fraudulent—rather, they think this applies only to a substantial minority of claimants.

### Should Spending on Benefits be Reduced or Raised?

The responses of a representative sample of the public to this question, which are set out in Table 2.3 reflect a marked difference in their attitudes to 'deserving' and 'undeserving' claimants.

Support for more social security spending on different groups of people declined across the board over the period 1998–2013. However, the most striking thing about the data in Table 2.3 is the marked difference in attitudes towards 'deserving' groups, such as those who care for the sick and disabled, parents on low incomes, disabled people who cannot work and retired people, on the one hand, and 'undeserving' groups, such as single

---

5    Department for Work and Pensions (2014).
6    Baumberg (2014).

**Table 2.3**  Attitudes to government spending on different claimant groups, 1998–2013

|  | 1998 (%) | 2002 (%) | 2004 (%) | 2006 (%) | 2008 (%) | 2011 (%) | 2013 (%) |
|---|---|---|---|---|---|---|---|
| *Would like to see more spending on* | | | | | | | |
| • people who care for sick and disabled | 82 | 82 | 81 | 82 | 83 | 74 | 73 |
| • parents who work on low incomes | 66 | 69 | 62 | 66 | 67 | 58 | 59 |
| • disabled people who cannot work | 72 | 69 | 63 | 62 | 61 | 53 | 54 |
| • retired people | 71 | 73 | 73 | 72 | 72 | 57 | 48 |
| • single parents | 34 | 39 | 35 | 36 | 37 | 29 | 31 |
| • unemployed people | 22 | 21 | 15 | 16 | 14 | 15 | 15 |
| *Would like to see less spending on* | | | | | | | |
| • people who care for sick and disabled | 1 | 1 | 1 | 1 | 1 | 1 | 1 |
| • parents who work on low incomes | 3 | 4 | 4 | 4 | 4 | 5 | 5 |
| • disabled people who cannot work | 2 | 2 | 3 | 3 | 4 | 5 | 4 |
| • retired people | 2 | 2 | 2 | 2 | 2 | 3 | 7 |
| • single parents | 21 | 18 | 18 | 19 | 17 | 21 | 19 |
| • unemployed people | 35 | 36 | 44 | 45 | 54 | 51 | 49 |

*Source* Baumberg (2014: Fig. 6.3)

parents and unemployed people, on the other. In 2013, only 15% of the public wished to see more spending on social security for the unemployed while more than three times as many (49%) favoured less spending.

What are we to make of all the data in Tables 2.1, 2.2, and 2.3? There was clearly considerable support for benefit sanctions if they left claimants with enough to cover their 'basic needs', and not a great deal of sympathy for unemployed claimants. Opinion on whether they received enough to live on was split (44% vs 44%); one third (33%) agreed with the statement that many social security claimants did not deserve help. Small majorities believed that unemployment benefits discourage work (57%) and that most unemployed claimants could find a job if they wanted to (54%) but as many as three in four believed that unemployed people fiddled the system in one way or another (77%). Less than one in six (15%) of people would have liked to see more spending on the unemployed people while one in two (49%) said they would like to see less spending. A lack of concern with benefit sanctions reflected a widely-shared lack of sympathy for unemployed claimants.

## Conclusion: Why Are Benefit Sanctions not a Matter of Greater Public Concern?

It will be argued in this book that benefit sanctions are ineffective and disproportionate, cause a great deal of injustice, are incompatible with the rule of law, and are, in no way, fit for purpose. However, because those who are subject to sanctions in the UK are blamed and regarded as responsible for what has happened to them, and because there is no organisation that has succeeded in drawing attention to the injustice associated with benefit sanctions and to the suffering they cause, there is relatively little recognition that they constitute a social problem. The callous and inhumane treatment of sanctioned claimants is not unlike that experienced by asylum seekers, immigrants, foreign-born spouses and other long-term residents who fail to produce evidence supporting their right to remain in the UK. Their experiences are well documented in the quality press but, in spite of the sense of outrage generated by these press reports, no heads have rolled, neither Ministers nor civil servants have been held responsible, and policies have been unaffected. The main reason for this is that, like those who are subject to benefit sanctions in the UK, there is little sympathy for asylum seekers, or for immigrants of any description, who are widely regarded as undeserving.

## References

Baumberg, B. (2014). Benefits and the Cost of Living. Pressures on the Cost of Living and Attitudes to Benefit Claiming. In *British Social Attitudes 31*. Available at http://www.bsa.natcen.ac.uk/media/38191/bsa31_benefits_and_the_cost_of_living.pdf.

Crowson, N. (2012). Revisiting the 1977 Housing (Homeless Persons) Act: Westminster, Whitehall and the Homelessness Lobby. *Twentieth Century British History, 24*(3), 424–447.

Department for Work and Pensions. (2014). *Fraud and Error in the Benefit System: 2012/13 Estimates (Great Britain)*. Available at https://assets.publishing.service.gov.uk/government/uploads/system/uploads/attachment_data/file/271654/fraudand-error-in-the-benefit-system-2012-13_estimates-160114.pdf.

Jones, E. (2016, May 23). Ken Loach Takes on Welfare System in I, Daniel Blake. *BBC News*, 23.

Ryan, W. (1971). *Blaming the Victim*. New York: Pantheon Books.

CHAPTER 3

# The Historical Development of Benefit Sanctions in the UK

This chapter provides an account of the development of eligibility and entitlement conditions and benefit sanctions in the UK following the introduction of unemployment insurance in 1911. Although, since then, unemployed people have had to meet a set of conditions to qualify for benefit and have been penalised for not meeting them, job search requirements and benefit sanctions only became an issue some 20 years ago. The chapter focuses on the period following the introduction of Jobseeker's Allowance (JSA) in 1996 and the New Deal in 1998. The developments described in the chapter reflect a shift away from an approach, in which the main function of social security was to prevent hardship, towards an approach, in which the main function of social security is to 'activate' unemployed people and get them back into work. This shift has involved the integration of social security policies and employment policies, which were formerly relatively autonomous policy areas. Although policies for the unemployed have always combined *passive* and *active* features, a largely 'passive' approach was in the ascendancy until the late 1980s while a more 'active' approach has increased in importance since then. The chapter concludes with an account of the current sanctions regime that was introduced in 2012.

© The Author(s) 2018                                                     21
M. Adler, *Cruel, Inhuman or Degrading Treatment?*, Palgrave
Socio-Legal Studies, https://doi.org/10.1007/978-3-319-90356-9_3

## THE BASIC NARRATIVE

The focus in this chapter is on the changing role of eligibility and entitlement conditions and benefit sanctions in unemployment protection schemes. The basic narrative is as follows. When unemployment benefit was introduced under the National Insurance Act 1911, claimants could be disqualified from benefit for periods of up to six weeks for one of for four reasons (if they were unemployed because of a labour dispute, if they were dismissed from their previous job for 'misconduct', if they left their previous job voluntarily and without 'just cause', or if they refused, 'without good cause' to apply for or take up a suitable job or training opportunity).[1] The maximum period of disqualification was increased to 13 weeks in 1986 and then to 26 weeks in 1988. Under the Restart Programme, introduced in 1986, everyone who had been unemployed for a year or more was invited to a Job Centre and offered one or more of eight positive opportunities designed to help them back into employment, with the threat of sanctions if they did not take part. The introduction of the Restart Programme, and the emphasis it placed on the claimant's behaviour, marked the beginning of the current benefit sanctions regime. By the end of the twentieth century, the number of sanctions imposed on recipients of benefit was between 130,000 and 150,000 per year. If disqualification decisions, that is decisions about whether an applicant was entitled to benefit in the first place, are also included, the combined number of sanctions and disqualifications was almost 300,000 per year.[2]

A series of social security reviews by the outgoing Conservative Government culminated in the introduction of Jobseeker's Allowance (JSA) in 1996, a pivotal change which intensified the monitoring of unemployed claimants' job-seeking behaviour. In 1998, the incoming Labour Government launched 'a new contract for welfare', which aimed to rebuild the welfare state around the work ethic, i.e. around the principle of 'work for those who can, security for those who cannot'.[3] This was followed by the introduction of several New Deal programmes in which 'Personal Advisers'[4] provided claimants with job-related advice and job-search assistance.

---

[1]   See Fulbrook (1978: 22).

[2]   Figures based on Employment Service Labour Market Statistics, Analysis of Adjudication Officers' Decisions for year ending 31 March 1999.

[3]   Published in 1998 principle was vigorously promoted by the Prime Minister (Tony Blair) and enacted in the Welfare Reform and Pensions Act 1999.

[4]   Now known as 'Work Coaches'.

Initially, participation in these programmes was voluntary for some groups, for example single parents and disabled people, and compulsory for others, for example young people and the unemployed, but, over time, participation became compulsory for more and more claimants. Under the three Labour Governments (1997–2001, 2001–2005 and 2005–2010), social security became increasingly conditional on meeting the job-search and administrative requirements of the New Deal programmes. This policy had cross-party support and was continued by the Coalition Government (2010–2015) and by the subsequent Conservative Government (2015).

Under the Work Programme, introduced in 2011, all job search activities were outsourced to external contractors on a payment-by-results basis.[5] This gave rise to concerns, denied by the DWP, that contractors increased the number of referrals to DWP decision-makers in order to concentrate on easy-to-place customers and meet their performance targets. The DWP paid Work Programme providers for the number of claimants who obtained permanent employment within a given period, typically 24 months.[6] The number of benefit sanctions continued to grow and peaked at over one million in 2013. Although it fell after that, the enhanced sanctions regime that was introduced in 2012 remained in place and has been carried forward into the Universal Credit (UC) scheme.

The basic narrative will be expanded in this chapter. Although it would have been instructive to explore how the formal rules dealing with eligibility and entitlement conditions and benefit sanctions were applied in practice, this has not been possible. Due to the unwillingness of the DWP either to carry out research itself or to grant access to external researchers to do so, no empirical research on implementation has been carried out in the UK. This is in marked contrast with the willingness of the Home Office to conduct its own research and to grant access to external researchers to conduct research on crime and policing.[7]

---

[5]  Margaret Hodge (2016), formerly Chair of the House of Commons Public Accounts Committee, provides a revealing account of the Work Programme, which draws attention to the failure of private contractors to achieve their targets despite receiving lucrative contracts from the government.

[6]  National Audit Office (2016: para 12).

[7]  The unwillingness of the Home Office to countenance research on immigration and asylum is, however, comparable to the unwillingness of the DWP to countenance research on social security and suggests that access is particularly difficult where it would focus on activities for which the government department is directly responsible.

## A BRIEF LOOK SIDEWAYS

Disqualifications and sanctions are not only to be found in unemployment benefit schemes but have also existed in sickness benefit schemes since the early twentieth century.[8] When the first statutory sickness benefit scheme was introduced in the UK, under the National Insurance Act 1911, it was administered by 'Approved Societies', for example by Friendly Societies, trade unions and private companies such as the Prudential Assurance Company. The Approved Societies were subject to strict statutory regulation but were entitled to make some of their own rules, including the power to regulate 'behaviour during sickness'. Societies were able to suspend benefit for up to twelve months, fine members up to ten shillings, or expel members from membership for breach of such rules.[9] Although the possibility of sanctions for sickness benefit claimants has been available since 1948, they have only been used occasionally. Sanctions have, however, been applied to disability benefit claimants with some force since the introduction of Employment and Support Allowance (ESA) in 2008.[10]

## 'PASSIVE' AND 'ACTIVE' APPROACHES TO SOCIAL SECURITY

It is sometimes said of the Beveridge Report, which laid the foundations for the British welfare state, that it reflected a *passive approach* to social security. This is because it regarded the main aim of social security as being the prevention of poverty, which was referred to as 'the abolition of want' and which was identified as one of 'the five giants on the road to post-war reconstruction'.[11] In the case of those who were capable of work, an *active approach* would have aimed either to get them back to work or to prepare them for work and to discourage them from relying on benefits. The passive approach was the dominant one for more

---

[8]   *Disqualifications* are applied to claimants who do not qualify for benefit, e.g. because they have left work voluntarily, for misconduct or because they are not considered to be unemployed or disabled. *Sanctions*, which are the main concern of this book, are applied when claimants are considered to have failed to meet the conditions of entitlement to benefit, e.g. for not attending interviews or training schemes, for not putting enough effort into job search or refusing to apply for or accept a job.

[9]   Gulland (2017).

[10]   Discussed below.

[11]   The others were Disease, Ignorance, Squalor and Idleness.

than 40 years after the Second World War, but the influence of the active approach has increased over the last 30 years. It began to take hold in the late 1980s under the Conservative Governments of Margaret Thatcher and John Major. It was continued and considerably extended under the Labour Governments of Tony Blair and Gordon Brown. And it was promoted, with great enthusiasm, by the Coalition Government led by David Cameron.

This characterisation has been vigorously challenged on the grounds that social security policy in the UK, and elsewhere, has always involved a mixture of 'active' (labour market) and 'passive' (income replacement) measures[12] and there is much to be said in favour of this critique. The Beveridge Report proposed that 'all the principal payments [including unemployment benefit] will continue ... without test of means so long as the need lasts but will normally be subject to a condition of attendance at a work or training centre'.[13] In other words, unemployment benefit would last for the duration of unemployment, but unemployed claimants could be required to attend a labour exchange if they wanted to carry on receiving benefit. Nevertheless, there has clearly been a change of emphasis.

Following the example of the Reagan administration in the US in the early 1980s, the Thatcher Government adopted an increasingly neoliberal approach to policy.[14] Employment rights were curtailed, and benefit levels were reduced. After the 1987 general election, the Conservative Government's approach to the unemployed and the welfare state changed quite dramatically. The overall aim of policy became that of reducing so-called 'welfare dependency' by restricting eligibility, policing the job-seeking behavior of the unemployed more closely and getting people off benefit.

A much stricter benefits regime was introduced. Conditions were imposed on claimants who failed to secure employment and the use of sanctions for those who did not satisfy the conditions was stepped up. However, 'carrots' were used as well as 'sticks'. 'In-work benefits' for the low-paid were promoted and unemployed claimants were given an in-work benefit assessment, involving an assessment of their entitlement to Family Credit (for those with dependent children), Housing Benefit (for tenants),

[12] See, for example, Sinfield (2001).
[13] Beveridge (1942: para 20).
[14] See King (1987) and Deacon (2000).

and Council Tax Benefit (for those who paid Council Tax),[15] alongside a review of their job-seeking activities. These measures were intended to ameliorate the unemployment trap[16] and encourage individuals to take low-paid jobs of the sort that were increasingly being generated in the deregulated labour market. The number of low-income households claiming family credit exceeded 500,000 in 1994 and, as a result, more than 2% of the workforce had their wages supplemented in this way.

## The Jobseeker's Act 1995

In 1995, the Major Government introduced legislation (the Jobseekers Act 1995) that led to the introduction of the Jobseeker's Allowance (JSA). JSA was a single benefit with unified rules that replaced a combination of contributory Unemployment Benefit and means-tested Income Support (IS) for the unemployed. Most unemployed 16- and 17-year-olds lost the right to benefit and were instead offered a place on a Youth Training Scheme (YTS). In addition, the benefit claims of those above that age, particularly the long-term unemployed, were scrutinised more rigorously. The previous requirement that claimants should be 'available for work' was supplemented by a stronger requirement that they should 'actively seek work'.

A key development in policies for those who were out of work was the shift towards making access to all social security benefits more conditional on work related criteria.[17] Until this point, compulsory employment advice and job-search assistance interviews was only

---

[15] These are all means-tested benefits for low income households. Family Credit, which was replaced by Working Families Tax Credit in 1999, was paid to working families who were responsible for at least one child under 16 (or under 19 if in full-time education) where the applicant or the applicant's partner (if they had one) worked for 16 hours or more per week. Housing Benefit is for low income households, who may either be on benefit or in work and who need financial help to pay all or part of their rent. Council Tax Benefit is likewise for low income households, who may be on benefit or in work and need financial help to pay all or part of their council tax, which is a local tax on domestic property that is paid by everyone who owns or rents their accommodation.

[16] The *unemployment trap* refers to the lack of financial incentives for unemployed people to return to work. It is caused by high replacement rates, i.e. by incomes for the unemployed that approach (and, in a few cases, exceed) the incomes they did or could obtain from work.

[17] Wright (2009: 200).

required for the unemployed but, since then, there has been an intensi-fication of the idea that other types of recipient should also be expected to look for work. When Jobcentre Plus was created in 2002, through a merger of the Employment Service with the Benefits Agency, a one-stop shop for everyone who was out-of-work benefits was created. All new claimants were provided with advice and information about training and encouraged to agree on a course of action. In addition, everyone in receipt of JSA was required to enter into a 'Jobseeker's Agreement', which specified the detailed weekly steps they were expected to take in looking for work.

All claimants were assigned to a 'Personal Adviser' whose role was to provide individualised and continuous support. Personal Advisers were also responsible for monitoring compliance with the Jobseeker's Agreement at fortnightly intervals and referring cases to DWP deci-sion-makers in local offices if they thought that the claimant had not met the terms of the Jobseeker's Agreement. DWP decision-makers were given the power to impose sanctions for work-related offences, e.g. for failure to apply for or refusal to accept a job vacancy. They also had the power to issue a 'Jobseeker's Direction', which required those in receipt of JSA to look for jobs in specified ways, take prescribed steps to 'improve their employability' or take part in a training scheme, and were also empowered to impose sanctions on those who did not meet these requirements.

When the Labour Party returned to government in 1997, it did not attempt to put back the clock but set out to develop a new 'Third Way' which incorporated some of the neo-liberal ideas that had been put in place by the Conservatives, while ostensibly maintaining its social demo-cratic commitment to social justice.[18] Its centrepiece was the New Deal, a set of policies that the new government announced in its first budget in 1997.[19] The avowed aim of the New Deal was to do everything possi-ble to get young people, the long-term unemployed, single parents and some of the long-term sick and disabled into work, in the belief that, for those who were able to work, work was the best guarantor of welfare.

In parallel with the New Deal, in an effort to ensure that 'work pays' and that people earned more in work than on benefits, the new Labour Government introduced a raft of other measures. These included the

[18] Giddens (1998).

[19] For an excellent review of the measures introduced by successive governments since 1997, see Wright (2009).

introduction (for the first time in the UK) of a national minimum wage, reductions in tax and national insurance contributions for low-paid workers and the launch of an ambitious pair of tax credits,[20] comprising Working Families Tax Credit (WFTC) and Disabled Person's Tax Credit (DPTC), which were introduced in 1999. These were replaced in 2003 by Working Tax Credit (WTC), which incorporated the adult components of WFTC and DPTC, and Child Tax Credit (CTC), which brought all child-related payments apart from Child Benefit into a single system. As a result, the child premiums in JSA were abolished. Over time, expenditure on tax credits for people in work grew at the expense of expenditure on benefits for non-retired people who were out of work.

As far as the New Deal was concerned, a distinction was made between two categories of unemployed claimants. The first category included claimants who were deemed able to work. The principle of *activation* was applied to them and they were to be helped and/or cajoled into work by one of six New Deal programmes—the New Deals for Young People (under 25), for those aged 25+ (formerly the New Deal for the Long-Term Unemployed), for the Partners of the Unemployed, for Disabled People, for Single Parents and for those aged 50+.[21] The second category included claimants excused from work, who continued to receive 'unconditional' support in the form of social security benefits. The principle of activation was not applied to them at this stage, although, as discussed below, it was extended to some of them later. A key feature of the New Deal, which distinguished it from previous initiatives, was the provision of support tailored to the needs and circumstances of each of its client groups. Programmes were specifically tailored to the circumstances of target groups (e.g. young people and lone parents), with some distinctive features provided within each programme.

Administratively, as noted above, the New Deal reforms involved the establishment of a new agency known as Jobcentre Plus, which was given responsibility for paying benefits to the unemployed and helping them back into the labour market, either directly by getting them into employment or indirectly by providing training to improve their employability.

[20] See Adler (2004) and Millar (2003).

[21] The distinctive feature of activation programmes is that participation is obligatory for relevant target groups. Key examples of activation programmes are requirements on unemployed people to attend intensive interviews with employment counsellors, apply for job vacancies as directed by employment counsellors, independently search for job vacancies and vapply for jobs, accept offers of suitable work, participate in the formulation of an individual action plan and participate in training or job-creation programmes.

Its establishment reflected a new mode of 'joined up' government—in which all government departments were expected to communicate with each other and to act together effectively, efficiently and in a coherent fashion—which was a central plank of the first Blair Government's proposals for public sector reform. At the 'street-level',[22] i.e. at the interface with the public, the merger was associated with the introduction of an individualised service, in which 'Personal Advisers' would meet claimants to discuss their work aspirations and options; assist them in searching for jobs; explore their training needs and the availability of training programmes; advise them on childcare and the availability of specialist services, such as services for those with drug or alcohol dependency; and make indicative calculations about whether or not they would be better off in work or on benefit.

The government's approach led to some very authoritarian policies and practices. Governments have always sought to make political capital from social security fraud[23] and this contributed to the belief that fraud was much more widespread than was actually the case and to the lack of public concern with benefit sanctions that was discussed in Chapter 2.[24] The widespread use of television advertising,[25] which encouraged the public to treat those in receipt of social security with suspicion, reinforced the efforts of social security staff to get claimants off benefit and into work. This emphasis on work may have led to the stigmatising of people on benefit.

Many aspects of the regime that was developed to get unemployed people in receipt of JSA back into work, e.g. frequent attendance at work-focused interviews (WFIs), were subsequently applied to those who, because of childcare responsibilities, illness or disability, were not in employment. This extension of the activation regime was intended to produce a shift in the boundary between those who can and those who cannot work. It was also assumed by the government that it would lead to a substantial reduction in the number of single parents and people registered as sick and disabled who were on benefit.[26]

---

[22]  See Lipsky (1980) and Wright (2003).

[23]  Sainsbury (2003).

[24]  See Chapter 1 above.

[25]  Members of the public are encouraged to report cases of *benefit fraud* to the National Benefit Fraud Hotline and the Department for Work and Pensions (DWP) employs over 3000 fraud investigators to investigate allegations of fraud and apprehend those who are involved. See Grover (2005).

[26]  For an account of these developments, and of the shift from a 'passive' to an 'active' approach in the provision of social security for sickness and disability, see Sainsbury (2009).

## THE WELFARE REFORM ACT 2007

Under the Welfare Reform Act 2007, policies were introduced with the aim of getting 1 million of the 2.7 million claimants who had been in receipt of Incapacity Benefit back into work. Incapacity Benefit, and IS paid on grounds of incapacity, were abolished for new claimants and replaced by the new ESA, with a much stricter test of disability. Thus, the new Work Capability Assessment (WCA) test aimed to assess what an individual *could* do, rather than what an individual *could not* do, and considered a person's capacities such as his/her ability to use a computer keyboard or mouse. Most claimants were required to complete a lengthy questionnaire about their condition and its effect on their ability to work and to attend a work-focused health-related assessment (WFHRA) with a health care professional[27] to assess their capability for work-related activities. Those who were deemed incapable of engaging in such activities were provided with a 'support component' while those who were deemed capable of doing so received a 'work-related activity component' and were required to participate in a series of WFIs with a Personal Adviser. Claimants who were assessed as not being able to take part in any work-related activity (the minority who were most severely disabled) were not required to take part in work-focused activities unless they wanted to and should therefore not have been at risk of being sanctioned. However, claimants who were assessed as being capable of taking part in some form of work-related activity (the majority who were less severely disabled) would be subject to sanctions if, without good cause, they did not attend or take part in a WFHRA or WFI.

### *Reviewing Conditionality and Sanctions*

In July 2008, the Secretary of State for Work and Pensions commissioned Professor Paul Gregg, an economist from the University of Bristol, to undertake a wide-ranging review of conditionality and sanctions, and to look at how more people could be transferred from benefits into work. The Gregg Report[28] recommended that all claimants should be allocated to one of three broad groups as follows:

---

[27] The health care professional may be a doctor, a nurse, an occupational therapist or a physiotherapist. From its inception, medical assessments for ESA were outsourced to private companies, first to Atos in 2008, and more recently to Maximus in March 2015.

[28] Gregg (2008).

- A 'Work-Ready' group for those who are immediately job-ready, who would be subject to standard job-search requirements like those in the JSA regime.
- A 'Progression to Work' group for those where an immediate return to work is unrealistic but where, with appropriate intervention, there is 'a genuine possibility' of a return to work.
- A 'No Conditionality' group, comprising those with a serious health condition or disability, single parents and partners whose youngest child is under the age of one, and certain carers, who would not be required to undertake work-related activities or to take steps to find work.

The Report presented data, reproduced in Table 3.1, on the incidence of referrals from Personal Advisers to DWP Decision-Makers and on sanctioning rates for the year ending August 2008. In this 12-month period, there were more than 800,000 referrals, and more than 500,000 sanctions were imposed on unemployed claimants—considerably more than the average annual number in the preceding years. This is partly because

**Table 3.1** Referrals from Personal Advisers to DWP decision-makers, disallowance rates and number of sanctions imposed over 12 months to August 2008

| Reason for the referral | Number of referrals | Disallowance rate (%) | Number of sanctions |
|---|---|---|---|
| Failure to attend an interview or appointment | 324,587 | 70 | 227,210 |
| Leaving a job voluntarily | 233,857 | 54 | 126,282 |
| Misconduct | 76,706 | 44 | 33,751 |
| Not actively seeking employment | 71,479 | 87 | 62,186 |
| Other reasons (including breach of jobseekers' directions and jobseekers' agreements) | 48,842 | 66 | 32,236 |
| Refusal of employment | 43,000 | 71 | 30,530 |
| Availability questions | 19,377 | 64 | 12,401 |
| Total | 817,848 | 64 | 524,596 |

*Source* Based on Gregg (2008: 71), author's calculations in italics

of the imposition of 227,000 sanctions for 'failure to attend an interview or appointment' but also because the sanctions regime as a whole had become more punitive.

According to the Gregg Report, sanctions were needed to underpin the obligations imposed on claimants and as a backstop for those who failed to meet them.[29] The Report claimed that, although the use of sanctions to enforce conditionality had been 'quite successful', it could be improved. It argued that the sanctions regime was too complex and too difficult to understand, that it was too time-consuming and too costly to operate, and recommended that it could be improved by:

- aligning the imposition of a sanction more closely with the behaviour that triggers the sanction and devolving decision-making for some key decisions to frontline staff, i.e. from DWP Decision-Makers to Personal Advisers;
- improving claimants' awareness and knowledge of what is required of them by introducing an early warning system for those at risk of being sanctioned, a stronger set of rules around attendance at mandatory meetings; and a move in the longer-term towards a system of fixed fines;
- dealing more effectively with repeat offenders by introducing a clear and simple sanction escalation procedure for all failures to attend an interview or appointment without good cause.

The Gregg Report was a rather one-sided document in that it focused on claimants' obligations to meet the requirements imposed on them by New Deal staff and was completely silent about the obligations of staff and whether or not they are successful in getting claimants, in particular 'hard-to-help' claimants, back into work or into training.[30] It was likewise silent on what claimants could do if they thought the sanctions imposed on them were unreasonable or if they were dissatisfied with what the staff had, or had not, done for them.[31] Although its commitment to greater transparency was welcome, the devolution of responsibility for imposing

---

[29]  Gregg (2008: 12).

[30]  There was likewise no discussion in the Report of whether the ECHR and other international conventions impose any constraints on what the New Deal authorities can require from claimants in return for the help that they are given.

[31]  See Gulland (2011).

sanctions from centralised decision-makers to front-line staff raised important questions of administrative justice and was very problematic.[32]

## THE WELFARE REFORM ACT 2009

As noted above, the principle of activation was first applied to unemployed persons who claimed JSA and was subsequently applied to the long-term sick and disabled individuals who claimed ESA. The Welfare Reform Act 2009 took this process further by setting out a framework for the abolition of IS and for moving those in receipt of IS to JSA or ESA. This was to apply to all single parents whose youngest child was aged seven and over—those who were thought to be able to work would be transferred to JSA and those who were sick or disabled to ESA. For them, the intention was to establish a conditionality regime tailored to their personal circumstances, so that preparation for work became a natural progression rather than a sudden step up. Single parents were to be required to undertake differing levels of activity, depending on the age of their youngest child. Where the child was less than one, no activity was to be required; where the child was between one and three, the parent would be required to attend a WFI at regular intervals; and where the child was between three and seven, the parent would be required to undertake work-related activity. Where conditions were set but not met and 'good cause' was not established, the appropriate sanction would be applied.

The government appears to have been concerned that the activation measures that were introduced into these benefit schemes had not been successful in getting 'problem drug users' back into work. Under the Welfare Reform Act 2009, those who claimed ESA were required to answer questions about their drug use, and claimants who did not declare that they were drug users but were suspected 'on reasonable grounds' of drug dependency or a 'propensity to misuse drugs' could be required to undergo a 'substance-related assessment'. Those who failed to comply with this requirement 'without good cause' could be required to undertake a test to ascertain the presence of drugs in the body.[33] Where the assessment suggested that the claimant had a

---

[32] This issue is discussed in Chapter 6.
[33] Harris (2010).

pattern of drug use that 'required and may be susceptible to treatment' and affected their job prospects, a 'rehabilitation plan' with a specialist employment adviser would be devised. This would specify the steps claimants were expected to take in order 'to stabilise their drug dependency, move towards recovery, tackle the problems they face and get into work'. Claimants were normally bound by the plan for 52 weeks and were expected to 'submit to treatment by or under the direction of a person having the necessary qualifications or experience', participate in interviews or assessments at places and times specified in the plan, and take any other specified steps. Sanctions could be imposed for non-compliance with any of the above requirements.

Drug users and the long-term sick and disabled were not the only claimants to have been affected by the shift towards greater conditionality and the increased use of sanctions for those who failed to satisfy the activation conditions that were imposed. Since 2000, all single parents on Income Support have been required to participate in WFIs[34] and, since 2008, they have had to undergo regular interviews every six months. Single parents who wished to take up the offer of greater support to move towards employment could volunteer for the New Deal for Lone Parents (NDLP) programme, which aimed to help them to improve their job readiness and employment opportunities and gain independence through working. This was achieved by accessing various forms of assistance and provision, which could be made available through a Personal Adviser.

## THE WELFARE REFORM ACT 2012

Universal Credit (UC), which was one of the Coalition Government's flagship pieces of social reform, was introduced under the Welfare Reform Act 2012. It is a single monthly payment for people in or out of work and was to have been introduced in 2013 to replace six means-tested benefits and tax credits: income-based JSA, income-based ESA, Income Support, Housing Benefit, WTC, and CTC. The plan was to introduce the new benefit gradually to all Job Centres, focusing initially on those claimants whose circumstances were the least complex.

---

[34] The requirement was phased in between 2001 and 2004. From April 2014, single parents whose youngest child is less the one year old have been exempted.

Universal Credit is a deceptively simple solution to what is arguably an unnecessarily complex system of means-tested support for people on low incomes. However, it has proved very much harder to implement than its proponents ever imagined.[35] Under the old system, the aim was to pay benefits within two weeks of a claim. Under UC, there is a formal waiting period of one week before people can claim, with the benefit paid monthly in arrears—the reason for this being that it was said to more closely mirror what it is like to be in a job. In practice, many people earning less than £10,000 a year are paid weekly. However, this provision results in an in-built wait of six weeks before people get their cash—three times as long as under the old system—and the DWP admits that, in around one fifth of cases, it is failing to meet even that target. Partly because of the demands for information it places on the claimants, waits of ten or twelve weeks are not uncommon.[36]

Pilots started in a few Job Centres around Manchester and, during 2013 and 2014, this pilot area gradually expanded to include the whole of North-West England and some other Job Centre areas. During 2015 and into 2016, UC was gradually rolled out across the whole of Great Britain for new claims from single jobseekers, and this process was completed on 27 April 2016. Since then, all new benefit claims by single jobseekers have been for UC rather than for benefits like JSA, ESA or IS. The intention is that, by September 2018, new claims by all groups of claimants will be for UC rather than for other benefits and that existing claimants of JSA, ESA and IS who have not had a change of circumstance will be transferred to UC from July 2019 with the process being completed in March 2022. However, there may be, and probably will be, further delays.

### The Increasing Use of Online Procedures

When UC was first rolled out in 2013, it used IT systems developed by private contractors in what were known as 'live service areas' and these were progressively rolled out in order to test and learn about processes and policy. Alongside these live service areas, the DWP built its own digital service system, which went live in a small number of areas in 2014.

---

[35] The original aim was to simplify an overcomplicated benefit system and ease the transition in and out of work and back again while ensuring, transparently, that it always paid to be in a job.

[36] Timmins (2016).

Between November 2014 and April 2016, further digital test areas were introduced and, from then onwards, the DWP has been rolling out the full digital service to existing live service areas in Great Britain. Claimants who are already claiming UC in these areas will eventually be transferred across to the digital service system although when and how this will happen is not yet clear. Once that process is complete, from July 2019, DWP will begin transferring claimants of other benefits to the full UC digital service with a view to completion by March 2022.

There are serious concerns that the 'digital by default' claims process, which is one of the key features of the online procedures used in the delivery of UC, is likely to make it more difficult for a wide range of citizens to claim their entitlements.[37]

## RECENT CHANGES IN CONDITIONALITY

A new, and stricter rule for unemployed benefit recipients was introduced in autumn 2011. Since then, all recipients of JSA have had to attend job-search reviews and to attend training programmes to confirm that they are available for and actively seeking work. Although the Unemployment Insurance Act 1921 had introduced a 'seeking work' test that required claimants to be 'actively seeking work and willing to accept employment paying a fair wage', this provision was not included in National Insurance Act 1946, which merely required unemployed claimants to be 'available for work', which they could demonstrate by appearing in person at the benefit office and 'signing on'. Daily commuting time was increased to '90 min each way' under the JSA regulations and claimants are now required to look for jobs within this parameter (and could be sanctioned if they did not accept them).[38]

The government has also made benefit sanctions tougher and the grounds for imposing them clearer, and did so, for recipients of JSA, ESA and for future recipients of UC, through separate sets of regulations under the 2012 Welfare Reform Act.[39] It made three main changes:

---

[37] For example, those with literacy problems or learning difficulties and those who don't, for whatever reason, have access to the internet. See Dwyer and Wright (2014).

[38] Langenbucher (2015).

[39] For details, see the Job Seeker's Allowance (Sanctions) (Amendment) Regulations 2012.

- **Scope**: More types of claimants were brought within the scope of conditions and sanctions. As described above, eligibility and entitlement conditions were tightened and benefit sanctions were applied to single parents to encourage them into work when their children were at a younger age. When UC was introduced, the scope of conditionality was expanded again and conditions and sanctions were introduced for low-paid workers to encourage them to increase their earnings.[40] Moreover, the sanctions rate for those on UC appears to have been considerably higher than that for those who remained on JSA.[41]
- **Severity**: It introduced a tiered system of sanctions with longer sanctions for more serious violations.[42]
- **Escalation**: It differentiated between first violations, second and third violations and increased the sanctions for recidivists.

The new sanctions regime that was introduced in 2012 is set out in Table 3.2.

Table 2.2 shows how the government distinguished between three levels of seriousness for sanctionable offences, between first offenders and recidivists, and between JSA and ESA claimants. It also increased the maximum length of a JSA sanction from six months to three years. The DWP was subsequently criticised by the National Audit Office for introducing these changes 'in ways that were difficult to predict' and for introducing 'new approaches with little evidence of their likely effect'.[43]

---

[40] Dwyer and Wright (2014).

[41] Between August 2015 and June 2017, the rate of sanctioning as a percentage of Universal Credit (UC) claimants subject to conditionality averaged 7.0% per month before challenges and was 5.2% in the three months from April–June 2017. It is not known how the sanctioning rate varies between the different groups who were on UC, although unemployed people accounted for 80.7% of UC claimants subject to conditionality at June 2017. Meanwhile, the JSA sanctioning rate stabilised at around 1.7 per month before challenges with the rates for ESA and for lone parents on Income Support much lower, averaging 0.3% per month. See Webster (2017). The contrasts in sanctioning rates are striking although why the sanctioning rate for UC claimants is so much higher than the sanctioning rate for JSA claimants is unclear.

[42] According to the National Audit Office, these changes moved the UK from eighth to third in the OECD rankings of unemployment sanction strictness. However, this is clearly incorrect.

[43] Comptroller and Auditor General (2016: para 1.13).

**Table 3.2** Sanction penalties introduced in 2012

| Sanction level | Applicable to | Description | Previous sanction regime | Revised sanction regime from October 2012 | | |
| --- | --- | --- | --- | --- | --- | --- |
| | | | | 1st failure | 2nd failure | 3rd failure |
| Higher level | JSA claimants | Failure to comply with the most important jobseeking requirements | Variable 1–26 weeks except MWA Fixed 13 weeks | 13 weeks | 26 weeks if within 52 weeks but not within two weeks of previous failure | 156 weeks if within 52 weeks—but not within two weeks—of previous failure that resulted in 26 or 156 week sanction |
| Intermediate level | JSA claimants | Failure to be available for work | Disentitlement but no sanction | Disentitlement then up to 4 weeks loss of benefit | Disentitlement then up to 13 weeks loss of benefit if within 52 weeks—but not two weeks—of previous entitlement ceasing | |

(continued)

**Table 3.2**  (continued)

| Sanction level | Applicable to | Description | Previous sanction regime | Revised sanction regime from October 2012 | | |
|---|---|---|---|---|---|---|
| | | | | *1st failure* | *2nd failure* | *3rd failure* |
| Lower level | JSA claimants | Failure to attend/ participate in an adviser interview/ training scheme | Fixed 1, 2, 4 or 26 weeks | 4 weeks | 13 weeks if within 52 weeks—of previous failure which resulted in a 4 or 13 week sanction | but not two weeks—of previous failure which resulted in a 4 or 13 week sanction |
| | ESA claimants in the Work Related Activity Group (WRAG) | Failure to attend/participate in an mandatory interviews or failure to undertake Work Related Activity | Open-ended 50% of Work— Related Activity Component (WRAC) for first 4 weeks, then 100% of WRAC | 100% of the prescribed ESA amount open-ended until re-engagement followed by a fixed period of 1 week | 2 weeks if within 52 weeks—but not two weeks— of previous failure | A weeks if within 52 weeks—but not two weeks— of previous failure which resulted in a 2 or 4 week sanction |

*Note* MWA = Mandatory Work Activity; WRAC = Work Related Activity Component; WRAG = Work Related Activity Group
*Source* Department for Work and Pensions (2013)

It has been suggested that the harsher sanctions regime that was introduced under the 2012 Welfare Reform Act can be explained in terms of the austerity measures that were introduced in response to the financial crisis which began with the collapse of the investment bank Lehmann Brothers in September 2008. However, although many other countries experienced a decline in their Gross Domestic Product (GDP), the UK was the only country among 40 countries in a recent OECD survey to increase the range of job-search requirements and the punitiveness of benefit sanctions.[44] This makes it clear that the UK Government's decision to increase the scope and severity of benefit sanctions in 2012 was a political decision rather than an economic one that cannot be explained simply in terms of austerity.[45]

As noted above,  UC is gradually replacing existing benefits like JSA, ESA and IS. The UC sanctions regime comprises four levels of sanction (lowest, low, medium and high) that escalate with the severity of the offence.[46]

1. **Lowest level**: These apply only if the claimant has to meet the work-focused interview requirement, and fails to attend or take part in a work-focused interview, and lasts until the claimant takes part in one.
2. **Low level**: They last until the claimant does whatever they were sanctioned for failing to do, plus 7 days for their first low level sanction in any 364 day period, 14 days for their second, or 28 days for their third if they:
   • fail to attend or take part in a work-focused interview, and a lowest sanction level does not apply;
   • fail to attend or take part in a training course; or
   • fail to take a specific action to get paid work, or to increase your earnings from work.
3. **Medium level**: Claimants will be sanctioned for 28 days for their first medium level sanction in any 364 day period, or 91 days for their second if they:

[44]  Langenbucher (2015: paras 44 and 51).
[45]  Adler and Terum (2018: 167–168).
[46]  Department for Work and Pensions (2018: Sect. 5).

- have to meet either the work search requirement—and fail to take all reasonable actions to find paid work or increase your earnings from work; or
- have to meet either the work availability requirement—and are not available to start work or attend interviews.

4. **Highest level**: Claimants will be sanctioned for 91 days for their first higher level sanction in any 364 day period, 182 days for their second, or 1095 days for their third if they:
   - have to meet the 'work preparation requirement' and fail to take part in Mandatory Work Activity;
   - have to meet the 'work search requirement' and fail to apply for a particular job when told to do so;
   - have to meet the 'work availability requirement' and refuse a job offer; or
   - leave work or reduce their hours of work, whether voluntarily or due to 'misconduct' (while claiming UC or just before their claim).

There are several other differences between UC sanctions and JSA sanctions.

- UC sanctions have been lengthened by making them consecutive, rather than concurrent;
- hardship payments have become repayable and their impact therefore lasts for much longer[47];
- the 80% hardship rate for 'vulnerable' JSA and ESA claimants no longer exists;
- UC claimants who are sanctioned must demonstrate 'compliance' for seven days before they can apply for hardship payments and must re-apply every four weeks.[48]

Although those who designed UC could, if they had wished, have made the sanctions regimes they inherited from the JSA and ESA less oppressive and more humane, they chose instead to do the opposite.

[47] Given that repayments are made at the rate of 40% of benefit—the same as the amount by which a hardship payment is lower than the benefit—this means that, for claimants receiving hardship payments, UC sanctions in effect last 3.5 times as long as their nominal length.

[48] For details, see Webster (2015c). Hardship payments are discussed in more detail in Chapters 5 and 6 below.

## Conclusion: What can be Learned from History?

The historical narrative presented in this chapter shows how, over the last 20 years, benefit sanctions have increased in scope and severity. Until the mid-1990s, they were largely backward-looking, their aim being simply to disqualify those who were deemed to be responsible for their own unemployment. However, since then, their main aim has been to discipline the unemployed, and other groups like long-term sick and disabled claimants and single parents, who have been swept up into the disciplinary net, to make it clear that being on benefit is a privilege rather than a right, that the privilege is associated with obligations and that those who fail to meet their obligations will have the privilege withdrawn. The chapter draws attention both to the fact that introduction of Jobseeker's Allowance in 1996 and the New Deal in 1998 represented something of a watershed, and to the striking continuity of approach between governments of different political colours (first Conservative, then, in succession, Labour, Coalition and again Conservative), all of which seem to have bought into the dominant ideology of conditionality.[49]

## References

Abercrombie, N., & Turner, B. S. (1978). The Dominant Ideology Thesis. *British Journal of Sociology, 29*(2), 149–170.

Adler, M. (2004). Combining Welfare-To-Work Measures with Tax Credits: A New Hybrid Approach to Social Security. *International Social Security Review, 57*(2), 87–106.

Adler, M., & Terum, L. I. (2018). Austerity, Conditionality and Litigation in Six European Countries. In S. C. Matteucci & S. Halliday (Eds.), *Social Rights in an Age of Austerity: European Perspectives* (pp. 147–177). London: Routledge.

Beveridge, W. (1942). *Social Insurance and Allied Services (Beveridge Report)*, Cmd. 6404. London: HMSO.

Comptroller and Auditor General. (2016). *Benefit Sanctions*, HC 628, Session 2016–17. London: National Audit Office. Available at https://www.nao.org.uk/wp-content/uploads/2016/11/Benefit-sanctions.pdf.

Deacon, A. (2000). Learning from the US? The Influence of American Ideas upon 'New Labour' Thinking on Welfare Reform. *Policy and Politics, 28*(1), 5–18.

---

[49] See Abercrombie and Turner (1978).

Department for Work and Pensions. (2013, September 10). *Jobseeker's Allowance: Overview of Revised Sanctions Regime.* Available at https:// www.gov.uk/government/uploads/system/uploads/attachment_data/ file/238839/jsa-overview-of-revised-sanctions-regime.pdf.

Department for Work and Pensions. (2018). *Guidance: Universal Credit.* London: GOV.UK. Available at https://www.gov.uk/government/publications/ universal-credit-and-you/universal-credit-and-you-a.

Dwyer, P., & Wright, S. (2014). Universal Credit, Ubiquitous Conditionality and its Implications for Social Citizenship. *Journal of Poverty and Social Justice, 22*(1), 27–35.

Fulbrook, J. (1978). *Administrative Justice and the Unemployed.* London: Mansell.

Giddens, A. (1998). *The Third Way.* Cambridge: Polity Press.

Gregg, P. (2008). *Realising Potential: A Vision for Personalised Conditionality and Support (The Gregg Review).* An independent report for the Department of Work and Pensions. Norwich: The Stationary Office. Available at http:// www.dwp.gov.uk/docs/realisingpotential.pdf.

Grover, C. (2005). Advertising Social Security Fraud. *Benefits, 13*(3), 199–205.

Gulland, J. (2011). Ticking Boxens: Understanding Decision Making in Employment and Support Allowance. *Journal of Social Security Law, 18*(2), 69–86.

Gulland, J. (2017). Working While Incapable to Work? Changing Concepts of Permitted Work in the UK Disability Benefit System. *Disability Studies Quarterly, 37*(4). Available at http://dx.doi.org/10.18061/dsq.v37i4.6088.

Harris, N. (2010). Reducing Dependency? Conditional Rights, Benefit Reform and Drugs. *Journal of Law and Society, 37*(2), 233–262.

Hodge, M. (2016). *Called to Account.* London: Abacus.

King, D. S. (1987). *The New Right: Politics, Markets and Citizenship.* Basingstoke: Macmillan Education.

Langenbucher, K. (2015). *How Demanding Are Eligibility Criteria for Unemployment Benefits—Quantitative Indicators for OECD and EU Countries* (OECD Social, Employment and Migration Papers, No. 166).

Lipsky, M. (1980). *Street-Level Bureaucracy: Dilemmas of the Individual in Public Services.* New York: Russell Sage Foundation.

Millar, J. (2003). From Wage Replacement to Wage Supplement: Benefits and Tax Credits. In J. Millar (Ed.), *Understanding Social Security: Issues for Policy and Practice* (1st ed., pp. 123–143). Bristol: Policy Press.

National Audit Office. (2016, November 17). *Benefit Sanctions: Detailed Methodology.* London: National Audit Office. Available at https://www. nao.org.uk/wp-content/uploads/2016/11/Benefit-sanctions-detailed-methodology.pdf.

Sainsbury, R. (2003). Understanding Social Security Fraud. In J. Millar (Ed.), *Understanding Social Security: Issues for Policy and Practice* (1st ed.). Bristol: The Policy Press.

Sainsbury, R. (2009). Sickness, Incapacity and Disability. In J. Millar (Ed.), *Understanding Social Security: Issues for Policy and Practice* (2nd ed., pp. 213–232). Bristol: The Policy Press.

Sinfield, A. (2001). Benefits and Research in the Labour Market. *European Journal of Social Security, 3*(3), 209–235.

Timmins, N. (2016). *Universal Credit: From Disaster to Recovery?* London: Institute for Government.

Webster, D. (2015c, November 18). *DWP Ad Hoc Statistical Release, JSA and ESA Hardship Applications and Awards: April 2012 to Jun 2015.* Available at http://www.cpag.org.uk/david-webster.

Webster, D. (2017, May 31). *Briefing: Benefit Sanctions Statistics: JSA, ESA, Universal Credit and Income Support for Lone Parents.* London: Child Poverty Action Group. Available at http://cpag.org.uk/david-webster.

Wright, S. (2003). The Street-Level Implementation of Unemployment Policy. In J. Millar (Ed.), *Understanding Social Security: Issues for Policy and Practice* (1st ed., pp. 235–253). Bristol: Policy Press.

Wright, S. (2009). Welfare to Work. In J. Millar (Ed.), *Understanding Social Security: Issues for Policy and Practice* (2nd ed., pp. 193–202). Bristol: Policy Press.

# CHAPTER 4

# Changes in the Scope, Severity and Incidence of Benefit Sanctions

This chapter compares the scope and severity of benefit sanctions before the introduction of Jobseeker's Allowance in 1996 and the New Deal in 1998 with their scope and severity after the introduction of the current sanctions regime in 2012. It also charts the rise and fall in the number of benefit sanctions that were imposed, which increased from 300,000 to 400,000 per year in the period 2001–2008 to more than 1,000,000 per year in 2013 before falling back to a little above their former level two years later. An attempt is made to explain what led to their rise and fall and to estimate the proportion of claimants who were sanctioned, which was considerably greater than the government's own estimate. The chapter concludes with an analysis of the administrative 'offences' that claimants are sanctioned for.

## CHANGES IN THE SCOPE AND SEVERITY OF BENEFIT SANCTIONS

In the first decade of the twentieth century, when disallowances were first introduced into unemployment insurance, they dealt mainly with the circumstances in which claimants lost their jobs and lasted for a maximum of six weeks. They were, in effect, disqualifications and were limited both in scope and in duration. Moreover, those who were disqualified from unemployment insurance still had a right to means-tested social assistance, initially from the Poor Law authorities and subsequently from the Unemployment Assistance Board (established in 1934), the National Assistance Board (established in 1948) and the Supplementary Benefits

© The Author(s) 2018
M. Adler, *Cruel, Inhuman or Degrading Treatment?*, Palgrave
Socio-Legal Studies, https://doi.org/10.1007/978-3-319-90356-9_4

Commission (established in 1966), albeit at a reduced rate.[1] Now sanctions are applied to the whole of the benefit the claimant receives. There is a residual system of discretionary 'hardship payments', which, for most claimants, are paid at 60% of normal entitlement to those who are literally destitute and have no other means of support, but the provision is an extremely residual one and sanctioned claimants are often not told about it.[2] Although 'vulnerable' claimants can apply immediately, most claimants are not allowed to apply for the first two weeks after the sanction is imposed and the DWP has itself acknowledged that that the two week wait will often damage the claimant's health.

To sum up, while sanctions used to be applied to unemployed people who were held to be responsible for losing their jobs, they are now much more concerned with the job-seeking behaviour of all claimants who are not in employment and with conformity to the administrative requirements that are imposed by Personal Advisers, now re-branded as Work Coaches, in 'welfare to work' schemes. They are most frequently imposed for not 'actively seeking work', for failure to participate in training or employment schemes and for missing interviews.[3]

The main changes in benefit sanctions over the last few decades are summarised in Table 4.1.

It is clear that benefit sanctions are now applied in more situations and last for much longer than they did in the recent past. Thus, they are considerably greater in *scope* and *severity*.

## CHANGES IN THE INCIDENCE OF BENEFIT SANCTIONS

As mentioned above, at the beginning of the twenty-first century, about 300,000 sanctions and disqualifications[4] per year were imposed by the DWP on JSA claimants. This figure remained at about this level for the

---

[1]  Immediately before the introduction of Income Support in 1988, the reduction was 40% of the scale rate for a single householder or non-householder.

[2]  See Department for Work and Pensions (2013: 162).

[3]  Webster (2014: 7). For a more detailed account, see below.

[4]  Since 2012, the published statistics no longer distinguish between sanctions and disqualifications and include both. However, a breakdown can be obtained by analysing the raw data. DWP Sanctions Statistics are available at https://www.gov.uk/government/collections/jobseekers-allowance-sanctions and the full dataset is in the Stat-Xplore database at https://stat-xplore.dwp.gov.uk/default.aspx. This refers to Great Britain, i.e. to England, Wales and Scotland and no statistics are available for Northern Ireland.

**Table 4.1**   Benefit sanctions before 1998 and since 2012[a]

| Before 1998 | After 2012 |
|---|---|
| Only passive—mainly for breach of eligibility conditions, e.g. for leaving work voluntarily, being dismissed for 'misconduct' or not being available for work | Also active—mainly for breach of entitlement conditions, e.g. for not 'actively seeking work', failing to attend a training or employment scheme, or missing an interview |
| Only applied to unemployed | Also applied to single parents and long-term sick and disabled people |
| Applied, primarily, to applicants for insurance benefits (UI) | Applied to applicants for and recipients of all the main out-of-work benefits (JSA, ESA and UC) |
| Applied for up to 6 weeks (1911–1986), 13 weeks (1986–1988) or 26 weeks (1988 onwards) | Now applied for periods ranging from 4 weeks to 156 weeks (three years) |
| Sanctioned claimants used to have a right to claim means-tested social assistance (at a reduced rate) immediately | Sanctioned claimants can now apply for discretionary 'hardship payments' (also at a reduced rate) but, in most cases, only after a two-week delay[b] |

[a]1998 was chosen as the first threshold because it was the year in which the New Deal programmes, involving a much greater commitment to conditionality, were introduced and 2012 as the second threshold because it was the year in which the current sanctions regime was introduced
[b]In Scotland, sanctioned claimants can apply for help from the Scottish Welfare Fund, the successor to the Social Fund in Scotland. See Simpson (2017)

next five years but started to rise quite sharply in 2006 and exceeded 1,000,000 in 2013. Thus, there was a 350% increase over the period 2001–2013. Although the DWP points out that the monthly sanction rate, that is the ratio of the number of JSA sanctions and disallowances imposed to the size of the JSA caseload had stabilised at about 6.5% of claimants per month before reviews/reconsiderations and appeals ('challenges'), and 5.5% after challenges, these figures seriously underestimate the incidence of benefit sanctions. A better measure would have been the proportion of those who claimed JSA who were sanctioned while on benefit, which was substantially higher. In addition to these JSA sanctions, from 2009 onwards, a smaller number of sanctions were imposed on recipients of ESA. The highest number recorded was about 37,000 in 2014. The detailed figures are set out in Table 4.2.

In 2014, the number of JSA and ESA sanctions imposed fell from just over 1 million in the previous year to just over 700,000. The main reason for this was the fall in unemployment and the corresponding reduction in the JSA caseload, which fell by 31%.

**Table 4.2**  JSA and ESA sanctions and disqualifications 2001–2016[a]

| Year | Number of JSA [and, since 2013, UC] sanctions and disqualifications imposed | % change since 2001 | Number of ESA sanctions and disqualifications imposed |
|---|---|---|---|
| 2001 | 300,104 | | |
| 2002 | 305,080 | +1.65 | |
| 2003 | 282,096 | −6.00 | |
| 2004 | 258,985 | −13.70 | |
| 2005 | 267,172 | −10.93 | |
| 2006 | 278,827 | −7.09 | |
| 2007 | 351,341 | +17.07 | |
| 2008 | 380,028 | +26.63 | |
| 2009 | 471,476 | +157.10 | 19,087 |
| 2010 | 742,030 | +247.26 | 30,298 |
| 2011 | 738,850 | +246.20 | 4817 |
| 2012 | 904,965 | +301.55 | 14,361 |
| 2013 | 1,037,000 | +345.55 | 34,022 |
| 2014 | 702,000 | +233.92 | 36,808 |
| 2015 | 358,000[b] | +19.29 | 24,500 |
| 2016 | 339,000[c] | +12.96 | 17,240 |

[a]Because no statistics were available for 2000, 2001 was selected as the base year for comparisons
[b]325,000 JSA sanctions plus 33,000 UC sanctions
[c]157,000 JSA sanctions plus 182,000 UC sanctions
Although some UC claimants were sanctioned since UC was introduced in January 2013, UC sanctions have only been reported since August 2015
*Source* The statistics are based on the DWP's quarterly sanctions statistics, published in *Jobseeker's Allowance and Employment and Support Allowance sanctions* and available at https://www.gov.uk/government/collections/jobseekers-allowance-sanctions

## REASONS FOR THE RISE AND FALL OF BENEFIT SANCTIONS

As shown in column 2 of Table 4.3, the UK unemployment rate was quite stable over the period 2001–2008, averaging just over 5% of the workforce. Following the financial crisis in 2008, it rose by about 50% to 7.5–8% of the workforce during the five years 2009–2013 before falling back to a level below that recorded for 2001. In 2017, it was at its lowest recorded level (4.3% of the workforce) since 1975.

Over the period 2001–2013, JSA sanctions increased by 350% and in the period 2013–2016, they decreased by 67%.

The figures set out in Table 4.3 show very clearly that, over the period 2001–2009, annual changes in the number of sanctions imposed reflected annual changes in the number of unemployed people on benefit. After that, annual changes in the number of sanctions imposed raced ahead.

**Table 4.3** Unemployment, claimant count and JSA sanctions, 2001–2016[a]

| Year | Unemployment rate (annual average) (%) | Claimant count (annual average) | % change since in claimant count since 2001 | Number of sanctions imposed | % change number of sanctions imposed since 2001 |
|---|---|---|---|---|---|
| 2001 | 5.1 | 969,900 | | 300,104 | |
| 2002 | 5.2 | 946,600 | −2.38 | 305,080 | +1.65 |
| 2003 | 5.0 | 933,000 | −3.80 | 282,096 | −6.00 |
| 2004 | 4.8 | 853,300 | −12.02 | 258,985 | −13.70 |
| 2005 | 4.8 | 861,800 | −11.15 | 267,172 | −10.93 |
| 2006 | 5.4 | 944,900 | −2.58 | 278,827 | −7.09 |
| 2007 | 5.3 | 864,500 | −10.87 | 351,341 | +17.07 |
| 2008 | 5.7 | 906,100 | −6.58 | 380,028 | +26.63 |
| 2009 | 7.6 | 1,527,700 | +57.51 | 471,476 | +57.10 |
| 2010 | 7.9 | 1,496,400 | +54.28 | 742,030 | +147.26 |
| 2011 | 8.1 | 1,534,300 | +58.19 | 738,850 | +146.20 |
| 2012 | 8.0 | 1,505,600 | +62.07 | 904,965 | +201.55 |
| 2013 | 7.6 | 1,424,300 | +55.23 | 1,037,000 | +245.55 |
| 2014 | 6.2 | 1,036,000 | +6.81 | 702,000 | +133.92 |
| 2015 | 5.4 | 743,348[a] | −18.74 | 358,000[c] | +19.29 |
| 2016 | 4.9 | 773,435[b] | −20.19 | 339,000[d] | +12.96 |

[a]681,000 JSA claimants plus 62,348 UC claimants
[b]452,353 JSA claimants plus 321,082 UC claimants
[c]325,000 JSA sanctions plus 33,000 UC sanctions
[d]157,000 JSA sanctions plus 182,000 UC sanctions
*Source* Unemployment rates based on the Labour Force Survey (LFS); claimant count based on administrative data from DWP; sanctions data based on the DWP's quarterly sanctions statistics

It should come as no surprise that the number of unemployed persons in receipt of benefit should reflect the unemployment rate. This number is known as the 'total claimant count' and was likewise quite stable over the period 2001–2008, averaging about 910,000 claimants. It then rose rapidly to more than 1,500,000 in 2009 and remained at this level for the next five years. It started to fall in 2014 and in each of the years 2015–2016 was below the level it had been at in the period 2001–2008. Since 2013, the DWP has been transferring unemployed claimants from income-based JSA to Universal Credit (UC) and, in April 2017 there were 706,110 unemployed claimants, of whom 483,355 were on JSA and 312,755 on UC.[5]

[5] Webster (2017b).

The number of sanctions imposed followed a similar pattern. It fluctuated slightly on a year-to-year basis over the period 2001–2008, averaging just over 300,000 sanctions per year, reached 700,000 in 2010 and exceeded 1,000,000 in 2013 before falling back to 700,000 in 2014. In 2015 it was 20% above its 2001 level and, in 2016, 10% above that level. Thus, it is clear that the rise and fall in the number of benefit sanctions reflected the rise and fall in the unemployment rate and in the claimant count. However, it is also clear that decreases in the number of sanctions imposed during the period 2012–2016 were proportionately much less than the decreases in the claimant count. Clearly, something else was going on.[6]

When the Coalition Government came to power in May 2010, there was an unannounced change of policy by ministers to pressurise DWP staff to make more referrals for JSA sanctions. The increase and then decline in the Work Programme, the flagship welfare-to-work scheme of the Coalition Government, in which the task of getting the long-term unemployed into work was outsourced to a range of public sector, private sector and third sector organisations, also played a part in the rise and fall of benefit sanctions, not least because of a ruling by ministers that contractors had to refer claimants to a DWP decision-maker for sanctioning in the case of any breach of requirements, even where they knew that the claimant was cooperating fully. Latterly, the number of new referrals to the Work Programme was reduced and the practice was officially discontinued in April 2017. It will be noted that this coincided with a decline in the number of sanctions imposed.

In trying to make sense of the figures in Table 4.3, it should be noted that the claimant count is an annual average, i.e. it represents the average number of individuals claiming benefit every month. However, the number of sanctions imposed is an annual total, i.e. it is the sum of the number of sanctions imposed during the year. This difference has implications for the calculation of sanction rates.

The data in Table 4.4 refer to the monthly average claimant count, i.e. the monthly average number of unemployed claimants in receipt of benefit (column 2) and to the annual number of sanctions imposed (column 3). The monthly average number of sanctions imposed has been calculated (column 4) and the ratio of the monthly average number of sanctions imposed to the monthly average claimant count computed (column 5).

[6]    A fuller account of the rise and fall of benefit sanctions can be found in Webster (2016b).

**Table 4.4** Crude and adjusted JSA/UC sanction rates, 2001–2016

| Year | Claimant count (monthly average) | Number of sanctions imposed (annual total) | Number of sanctions imposed (average monthly total) | Crude sanctions rate (%) | Adjusted sanctions rate (%)[a] |
|------|------|------|------|------|------|
| 2001 | 969,900 | 300,104 | 25,009 | 2.50 | 7.02 |
| 2002 | 946,600 | 305,080 | 25,423 | 2.69 | 7.02 |
| 2003 | 933,000 | 282,096 | 23,508 | 2.52 | 7.32 |
| 2004 | 853,300 | 258,985 | 21,575 | 2.53 | 6.41 |
| 2005 | 861,800 | 267,172 | 22,264 | 2.58 | 6.38 |
| 2006 | 944,900 | 278,827 | 23,235 | 2.46 | 6.42 |
| 2007 | 864,500 | 351,341 | 29,278 | 3.39 | 7.16 |
| 2008 | 906,100 | 380,028 | 31,669 | 3.50 | 8.94 |
| 2009 | 1,527,700 | 471,476 | 39,290 | 2.57 | 7.84 |
| 2010 | 1,496,400 | 742,030 | 61,836 | 4.13 | 7.73 |
| 2011 | 1,534,300 | 738,850 | 61,571 | 4.01 | 12.09 |
| 2012 | 1,505,600 | 904,965 | 75,414 | 5.01 | 10.17 |
| 2013 | 1,424,300 | 1,037,000 | 86,417 | 6.07 | 13.83 |
| 2014 | 1,036,000 | 702,000 | 58,500 | 6.03 | 16.68 |
| 2015 | 797,800 | 358,000 | 29,833 | 3.74 | n.a. |
| 2016 | 774,100 | 339,000 | 28,250 | 3.65 | n.a. |

[a]No figures were provided for 2015 or 2016
*Source* Claimant count based on administrative data from DWP; sanctions data based on the DWP's quarterly sanctions statistics. Adjusted sanctions rates taken from Malik (2015)

This will be referred to as the 'crude sanctions rate'. It will be seen that this gradually increased from just over 2.5% in 2001 to 5% in 2012 and 6% in 2013 before falling back to a level between 3.5 and 4% in 2015 and 2016. If there were no changes in claimant behaviour, this would suggest that the sanctions regime became stricter over the period and that, in the period 2012–2014, it was twice as strict as it had been a decade earlier. The crude sanctions rate figures suggest that, since 2014, the sanctions regime has become less strict but that it is still stricter than it was in the early 2000s.

## THE PROPORTION OF JSA CLAIMANTS WHO ARE SANCTIONED

For a long time, ministers and officials claimed that only a 'tiny minority' of JSA claimants were sanctioned. They supported this assertion by comparing the number of sanctions that were imposed each month, after reviews/reconsiderations and appeals, with the number of claimants.

This ratio fluctuated between 2.5 and 6% in the period between 2000 and 2016. The number of sanctions that were imposed each month before reviews/reconsiderations and appeals is somewhat higher and would have been a better measure because everyone who receives a sanction experiences a period without benefit. However, neither of these measures is at all satisfactory. The proportion of claimants who are sanctioned increases as they spend longer on benefit and a better measure would be the proportion of claimants who are sanctioned in the course of a single claim for benefit. This comprises claimants who are sanctioned in the first month of claiming, in the second month of claiming and so on, until their period on benefit ends. 'Adjusted sanction rates', which use this measure and incorporate a number of other adjustments, are listed in column 6.[7] They are consistently higher than the rates published by the DWP and, because they measure the proportion of claimants who are sanctioned in the course of a year, are much more meaningful than the DWP figures.

In February 2014, in response to a Freedom of Information (FOI) request,[8] DWP provided information for the first time on the proportion of JSA claimants who had been sanctioned and the number of repeat JSA sanctions that had been imposed.[9] Almost one-fifth (18.4%) of the 3,097,630 individuals who claimed JSA during 2013–2014 were sanctioned, a total of 568,430 people. The figure of 18.4% for the proportion of JSA claimants in 2013/2014 who were sanctioned was the highest recorded until then. The proportion of JSA claimants sanctioned in the six previous years is set out in Table 4.5.

It should be recalled that these figures show the proportion of claimants sanctioned after reviews/reconsiderations and appeals. The proportion receiving a sanction before these challenges in 2013–2014 would have been higher, probably by about 20%.

The DWP's response to the FOI also revealed that 22.3% of the 8,232,560 individuals who claimed JSA over the five-year period 2009–2010 to 2013–2014 inclusive, had been sanctioned, a total of 1,833,035 people. This is after reviews-reconsiderations and appeals and the

---

[7]  Malik (2015) provides a very good critique of the crude sanctions rate statistics used by the DWP and a very clear account of how an adjusted sanctions rate can be calculated.

[8]  Freedom of Information request 2014-194, 14 February, reported in Webster (2015a).

[9]  See Webster (2015a).

**Table 4.5** Proportion of JSA claimants sanctioned, 2007/2008–2015/2016

| Year | Proportion of JSA claimants sanctioned (%) |
|------|--------------------------------------------|
| 2007–2008 | 11.8 |
| 2008–2009 | 9.8 |
| 2009–2010 | 10.8 |
| 2010–2011 | 15.1 |
| 2011–2012 | 13.2 |
| 2012–2013 | 16.0 |
| 2013–2014 | 18.4 |
| 2014–2015 | 14.1 |
| 2015–2016 | 8.2 |

*Source* See Webster (2015a: 6)

proportion receiving a sanction before these challenges must have been about 25%.[10] The average number of sanctions per sanctioned claimant over those five years, after reviews/reconsiderations/appeals, was 1.95. These figures make it clear that the 'tiny minority' of JSA claimants who received a sanction that ministers and officials referred to was only a fraction of a more reliable and meaningful figure and a gross under-estimate of the actual proportion.

A further FOI request[11] produced data for 2014–2015 and 2015–2016 that have been incorporated into Table 4.5. Not surprisingly, in view of the large fall in the number of claimants, there has been a corresponding fall in the proportion sanctioned each year, which fell from a peak of 18.4% in 2013–2014 to 8.2% in 2015–2016, lower than in any year since this measure became available.

The first FOI request referred to above indicated that, disregarding any distinctions between levels of sanction, of the 539,225 individual JSA claimants who were sanctioned in the year to June 2014, 166,764 (30.9%) were sanctioned more than once, and 67,143 (one in eight or 12.5%) were sanctioned three or times or more.

---

[10] Based on a re-analysis of Departmental data, the National Audit Office has calculated that 24% of claimants who were in receipt of Jobseeker's Allowance at any point between 2010 and 2015 received a sanction, of whom 58% received one sanction, 20% received two and 22% received three or more. See Comptroller and Auditor General (2016: Fig. 5).

[11] Freedom of Information request 2017-965, 6 April, reported in Webster (2017a).

## WHAT OFFENCES ARE SANCTIONS IMPOSED FOR?

Benefit sanctions can be imposed for the following reasons:

- for 'not actively seeking work', which, according to the Claimant Commitment,[12] all JSA claimants and all unemployed UC claimants are required to sign, includes spending at least 35 hours a week looking for or preparing for work, providing evidence of their efforts to obtain employment and compliance with official requirements;
- for non-participation in a training or employment scheme under the Work Programme;
- for being late for, or failing to attend, an interview or meeting.

In fact, all of these are misnomers: 'not actively seeking work' usually means that the claimant is actively seeking work but has not done exactly what they have been instructed by the Job Centre, for instance in the way they filled in their job search record; 'non-participation in the Work Programme' usually means missing a single interview with the contractor; and 'failure to attend an interview' often means being slightly late.[13]

Figure 4.1 shows that the relative importance of these reasons has changed over the period 1997–2015.

In the early years, sanctions for leaving a job voluntarily or through misconduct were the main reason for receiving a sanction but their importance declined over the period and, in recent years, receiving a sanction for this reason has been relatively uncommon. Currently, the most common reasons for receiving a sanction are not taking part in a training or employment scheme; being late for or failing to attend an interview or a meeting; and not 'actively seeking work', i.e. not doing enough to look for work.

Figure 4.2 shows how the relative importance of these three reasons has changed over the period.

Until about 2012, failing to attend an interview was much the most common reason for receiving a sanction but, since 2012, with a bit of a

---

[12] The Claimant Commitment, introduced in 2013, is an individual action plan, broadly similar to the Jobseeker's Agreement, which specifies the work-related actions claimants are expected to take and includes details of the sanctions that may be applied for non-compliance.

[13] See Webster (2015b).

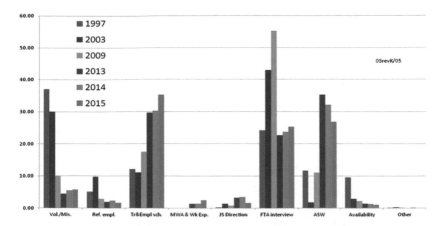

**Fig. 4.1**  Changing reasons for JSA sanctions, 1997–2015: the number of sanctions imposed for each reason as a percentage of the total number of sanctions imposed. *Note* Vol/Mis=sanctions for leaving a job voluntarily or through misconduct; Ref empl=sanctions for refusing employment; TR&Empl. sch=sanctions for not taking part in a training or employment scheme; MWA & Wk Exp=sanctions for not taking part in mandatory work activity or a work experience scheme; FTA interview=sanctions for being late or not turning up for appointments or interviews; ASW=sanctions for not actively seeking work; Availability=sanctions for not being available for work (*Source* Webster 2016a: Fig. 5)

glitch in 2014, the most common reason has been not taking part in a training or employment scheme.

Breaches of entitlement conditions, imposed for administrative offences committed by those who are already in receipt of benefit rather than breaches of eligibility conditions, imposed for unacceptable workplace behaviour from those wishing to claim benefit, are clearly the main reasons for being sanctioned. Although minor administrative failings, comparable to missing a medical appointment were, until a few years ago, the most important single reason for receiving a sanction, they have now been overtaken by offences related to job training and job search.

The Welfare Conditionality Project, funded for 5 years by the ESRC, has carried out an ambitious programme of research on conditional welfare in the UK, investigating the effects of sanctions and support measures in a number of poilicy areas on people's lives. They have interviewed 481 people living in Bath, Bristol, Edinburgh, Glasgow,

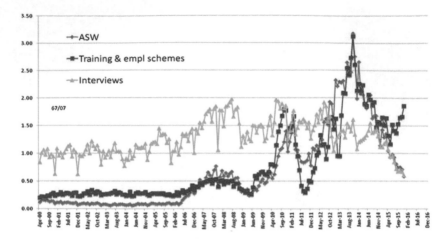

**Fig. 4.2** The average number of JSA sanctions (before challenges) for not taking part in a training or employment scheme, not 'actively seeking work' and being late for or failing to attend an interview or a meeting, as a percentage of the number of claimants, 2000–2016 (*Source* Webster 2016a: Fig. 6)

Greater Manchester, Inverness, London, Peterborough, Sheffield and Warrington, interviewing the same people three time to see what the longer-term effects of the sanctions and support measures are. Those who were interviewed included unemployed people claiming Jobseeker's Allowance, individuals and households claiming UC, lone parents, disabled people, social tenants, homeless people, people subject to antisocial behaviour orders or family intervention, migrants and offenders. They included 64 jobseekers of whom 34 had been sanctioned.

The interviews revealed that sanctions had a range of negative effects including shock and confusion (particularly for those who believed they had been compliant); financial hardship and deep poverty; debt, arrears, eviction threats and homelessness; food bank use; ill-health and severe and acute emotional effects, such as anxiety and depression. Most unemployed interviewees said that they were already keen to find work and did not need the threat or application of sanctions to spur them on to action that they were already taking.[14]

[14] Wright and Stewart (2016: 1).

Sanctions are intended to prompt behaviour change but most of the unemployed interviewees who had received a sanction reported that they were already keen to find work and contested the validity of their sanction: They also indicated that effective support was largely unavailable, since Jobcentre Plus focused on benefit claims and lacked the capacity to help with job-search. The main source of support was self-help via the online vacancy system, which some interviewees found 'quite easy' to use but others had difficulty with because of their lack of computer literacy or because of access problems. Most of the unemployed interviewees did not see the Work Programme or its associated courses and work placements as 'support'.[15]

The sample of 481 interviewees also included 58 disabled people, of whom 21 had experienced benefit sanctions, either when they were in receipt of ESA or earlier when they were in receipt of JSA. They made 'clear and repeated references to the negative impact of sanctions' both on their financial circumstances and on their physical and mental health.[16]

Two recent reports, both from Scotland, provide illustrations of the circumstances that gave rise to sanctions. The first comprises 91 accounts collected by a group of volunteers in Dundee[17] while the second comprises eight cases handled by Citizens' Advice Bureaux.[18]

Below is a selection of cases that gives a flavour of the circumstances that can result in a sanction. Many people had been sanctioned for missing meetings for which [according to them] they never received an appointment letter or for which the letter was sent out too late.

Allan (47) had been sanctioned twice by the Job Centre via Triage [the local Work Programme provider]. He was sanctioned for four weeks for missing a Triage appointment for which he did not receive a letter. When he did eventually receive the appointment letter, the date had already passed – and the letter was in fact dated the same day as his supposed appointment (it had been sent out on the same day he was supposed to attend). He asked about appealing his sanction but was told by Triage that this would not be possible. Allan was sanctioned a second time for twelve weeks for leaving early during a job-search meeting. (SUWN Case 19)

---

[15] Ibid.
[16] Dwyer et al. (2016: 8).
[17] Scottish Unemployed Workers' Network (2014).
[18] Citizens Advice Scotland (2012).

There were also many examples of benefits stopped due to clear administrative errors, such as lost forms, made by the Job Centre or the DWP.

> Kevin had been sanctioned twice, consecutively. He was told to apply for two jobs for kitchen and cleaning staff, which he duly did on the Government Gateway site. He subsequently received a letter saying that he had not applied for the jobs. He phoned to say that he had, and had proof on his on-line job-search record. But when he went to check his record, he discovered that the jobs had disappeared and simply showed up as 'no longer available'. He was sanctioned for 13 weeks, and the day we met him he had been informed that he had been sanctioned again, for six months, for the same thing. The Job Centre staff would not believe he was telling the truth, despite his partner having witnessed him apply for both positions. (SUWN Case 38)

Reasons for sanctions included the patently absurd—being unable to sign on through being at a job interview or on work experience.

> An East of Scotland CAB reported a client claiming joint JSA with her partner. They had both been sanctioned because her partner did not attend an interview which occurred when he was attending a mandatory work placement. The client's partner explained to the Job Centre that when he enquired about the double booking the work placement provider had advised him to attend the placement, rather than the interview, but the sanction was still imposed. (CAS Case 3)

A large number of examples demonstrate the inflexibility of the system and its failure to accommodate the restrictions and traumas of people's actual lives. These last include sanctions for missed appointments due to illness or bereavement—even a hospital stay and a father's funeral.

> Luke (40) was sanctioned in March when a family funeral clashed with his Triage appointment. He tried to contact Triage but without success. He got a letter from the DWP office in Clydebank asking for an explanation of the missed Triage appointment, and saying he would be sanctioned if he did not have a reasonable excuse. He wrote to them explaining about the funeral – and got sanctioned. (SUWN Case 61)

No allowance was given for those without computers or computer skills who were still expected to complete on-line searches and had to rely on finding a computer and assistance in their local library.

Jimmy (52) had only been receiving JSA for a month. He had recently been sanctioned by the Job Centre and did not know how long the sanction was going to last. He had been told that as part of his job search he must use the DWP's online Universal Jobmatch every day. He does not have a computer at home, is not terribly computer literate and has to book time at the library to use the internet. This is not always possible if it is fully booked. He was sanctioned for failing to use the internet every day. (SUWN Case 51)

Requirements for job searches and prospective work may fail to take account of mental or physical ill health.

Stuart (46) is a paranoid schizophrenic and suffers from depression. He is presently on ESA, and has been told he could get DLA but is nervous about applying. In the past he was sanctioned for two weeks for missing an appointment. He had been sent to Triage – and although his GP advised him not to go, he was afraid he would lose his benefits if he did not. He had passed two medical assessments in two years that appear to have taken little account of his mental health condition; and at one Triage session he was told 'if [he] felt paranoid, just to give a nod and he could go out of the room'. (SUWN Case 43)

The actions expected of claimants vary hugely (and apparently arbitrarily) and can be absurdly onerous, such as applying for 32 jobs every fortnight.

Robert (33) had gone back on JSA a month before we talked, having spent six months on ESA. He had been sanctioned in November 2013 for not meeting the requirements of his Jobseeker's Agreement. He had had to look for 32 jobs every two weeks and miscounted. He was sanctioned again in the same month for losing his job-search diary and using paper instead. (SUWN Case 64)

Although these accounts only record one side of the story, and this fact must be taken into account in assessing their validity, they point to a contrast between out-of-work claimants, who are as fallible and prone to error as the rest of us, and an insensitive rule-bound bureaucracy that is seemingly unable (or unwilling) to respond in sensible ways to human foibles and weaknesses, or to acknowledge its own errors.

## Conclusion: Benefit Sanctions Today

This chapter compares benefit sanctions before 1998, when the New Deal was introduced, with benefit sanctions since 2012, when the current sanctions regime was introduced. Although the comparison is a rather stark one, there can be little doubt that benefit sanctions have, over time, been applied to more administrative offences than in the recent past and that they now last for much longer than used to be the case. Thus, they are now considerably wider in *scope* and greater in *severity*. The chapter also accounts for changes in the *incidence* of benefit sanctions. It shows that the number of sanctions imposed reflected the number of unemployed people on benefit but that policy changes were also important. It also shows that the proportion of claimants who have been sanctioned was considerably higher than the official estimates indicated and presents some better estimates of the proportion of JSA claimants who have been sanctioned. These estimates suggest that the proportion of claimants receiving a sanction was about 20% (before challenges). It concludes by analysing the administrative offences for which sanctions are now imposed, the most common being not taking part in a training or employment scheme, being late for or failing to attend an interview or a meeting, and not 'actively seeking work'. In the criminal justice system, most of these offences would be classified as 'minor misdemeanours'. The accounts of the circumstances in which individual claimants have been sanctioned that were reproduced in the chapter provide ample evidence of this.

## References

Citizens Advice Scotland. (2012). *Voices from the Frontline: JSA Sanctions.* Edinburgh. Available at https://www.cas.org.uk/publications/voices-frontline-jsa-sanctions.

Comptroller and Auditor General. (2016). *Benefit Sanctions*, HC 628, Session 2016–17. London: National Audit Office. Available at https://www.nao.org.uk/wp-content/uploads/2016/11/Benefit-sanctions.pdf.

Department for Work and Pensions. (2013, September 10). *Jobseeker's Allowance: Overview of Revised Sanctions Regime.* Available at https://www.gov.uk/government/uploads/system/uploads/attachment_data/file/238839/jsa-overview-of-revised-sanctions-regime.pdf.

Dwyer, P., Jones, K., McNeill, J., Scullion, L., & Stewart, A. (2016). *First Wave Findings: Disability and Conditionality*. Available at http://www.welfare-conditionality.ac.uk/wp-content/uploads/2016/05/WelCond-findings-disability-May16.pdf.

Malik, S. (2015, August 5). Benefit sanctions: How estimated annual rates help scrutinise policy. *The Guardian.* Available at https://www.the-guardian.com/politics/datablog/2015/aug/05/benefit-sanctions-estimated-annual-rates-scrutinise-dwp-policy.

Scottish Unemployed Workers' Network. (2014, December). *Sanctioned Voices: A Report on the Impact of the DWP Sanctions Regime as Implemented in Dundee Job Centre, Compiled by Volunteers for the Scottish Unemployed Workers' Network.* Available at https://suwn.files.wordpress.com/2015/12/sanctioned_voices.pdf.

Simpson, M. (2017). Renegotiating Social Citizenship in the Age of Devolution. *Journal of Law and Society, 44*(4), 646–673.

Webster, D. (2014, November 12). *Briefing: The DWP's JSA/ESA Sanctions Statistics Release.* Available at http://www.cpag.org/david-webster.

Webster, D. (2015a, February 18). *Briefing: The DWP's JSA/ESA Sanctions Statistics Release.* Available at http://www.cpag.org/david-webster.

Webster, D. (2015b, May 13). *Briefing: The DWP's JSA/ESA Sanctions Statistics Release.* Available at http://www.cpag.org/david-webster.

Webster, D. (2016a, May 18). *Briefing: The DWP's JSA/ESA Sanctions Statistics.* Available at http://www.cpag.org/david-webster.

Webster, D. (2016b, October 3). *Supplement: Explaining the Rise and Fall of JSA and ESA Sanctions 2010–16.* Available at http://www.cpag.org/david-webster.

Webster, D. (2017a, February 22). *Briefing: The DWP's JSA/ESA Sanctions Statistics Release.* Available at http://www.cpag.org/david-webster.

Webster, D. (2017b, May 31). *Briefing: Benefit Sanctions Statistics: JSA, ESA, Universal Credit and Income Support for Lone Parents.* London: Child Poverty Action Group. Available at http://cpag.org.uk/david-webster.

Wright, S., & Stewart, A. (2016). *First Wave Findings: Jobseekers.* Available at http://www.welfareconditionality.ac.uk/wp-content/uploads/2016/05/WelCond-findings-jobseekers-May16.pdf.

# CHAPTER 5

# Conditionality and the Changing Relationship between the Citizen and the State

In this chapter, it is argued that conditionality should be understood as the primary or 'first-tier' concept, and that the two sides of conditionality, namely 'benefit conditions' and 'benefit sanctions', should be understood as 'second-tier' concepts. The chapter analyses the different ways in which conditions can be attached to the receipt of benefits and the nature of citizenship in the welfare state. It gives a good deal of attention to T.H. Marshall and his legacy and discusses the implications of Marshall's emphasis on rights rather than duties. It concludes with a discussion of recent attempts to recalibrate the balance between rights and responsibilities and of the central role played by conditionality in this process.

## THE TWO SIDES OF CONDITIONALITY

Conditionality refers to the attachment of conditions to the receipt of benefits or services and the imposition of sanctions on those who do not meet the conditions. It has been applied in some areas of social policy but not in others[1] and its application differs between countries.[2] The focus here is on conditionality in unemployment benefit schemes, broadly defined to include unemployment insurance (UI), unemployment assistance (UA) and social assistance (SA) schemes for

---

[1] See Watts et al. (2014).
[2] Langenbucher (2015).

© The Author(s) 2018
M. Adler, *Cruel, Inhuman or Degrading Treatment?*, Palgrave
Socio-Legal Studies, https://doi.org/10.1007/978-3-319-90356-9_5

unemployed people. Following Knotz and Nelson,[3] conditionality is regarded as the primary or 'first-tier' concept and comprises 'conditions' and 'sanctions', both of which may be regarded as 'second-tier' concepts.

As pointed out in Chapters 3 and 4, the receipt of unemployment benefit has always been subject to *eligibility conditions*. However, since the 1980s, a new set of conditions was introduced in many countries. With the adoption of active labour market policies (ALMPs), recipients of unemployment benefit have increasingly been expected to 'actively look for work' and benefit has only been awarded on the condition that they do so. The penalties for not doing so are known as benefit sanctions. These behavioural conditions, which refer to behaviour while in receipt of benefit, can be referred to as *entitlement conditions*, and, in different countries and at different times, they have varied in severity and duration. Entitlement conditions are more controversial than eligibility conditions and, over time, have become more prevalent.

## THREE FORMS OF CONDITIONALITY

This account resonates with Clasen and Clegg's analysis of welfare conditionality.[4] They distinguish between:

- **Conditions of category**, in which eligibility is conditional on membership of a defined category or group, e.g. being past retirement age for retirement pensions, having some form of disability for incapacity benefit, being unemployed for unemployment benefits and so on;
- **Conditions of circumstance**, in which eligibility criteria include or exclude individuals on the basis of their circumstances, e.g. their employment history, contribution record or their degree of financial need (assessed through a means-test);
- **Conditions of conduct**, in which entitlement criteria refer to meeting the behavioural requirements and constraints that are imposed upon different kinds of benefit recipient through legislation or administrative guidance. The most well-known example are

---

[3]  Knotz and Nelson (2013).
[4]  Clasen and Clegg (2007).

activation policies for the unemployed, under which unemployment benefit and unemployed SA recipients are obliged to provide evidence of job-search activities, participate in training programmes and/or agree to specialised counselling.

Each level of conditionality (category, circumstance, conduct) is associated with a set of levers (category definition, eligibility and entitlement criteria and behavioural requirements). Clasen and Clegg use this framework to compare the emphasis, direction and structure of national reform trajectories in the UK, Germany, France and Denmark over time.

As far as the UK is concerned, Clasen and Clegg argue that, during the 1980s and early 1990s when the unemployment rate was very high, policy focused on tightening conditionality at the first and second levels. The second level of conditionality was frequently and consistently tightened between 1980 and 1996 when Jobseeker's Allowance was introduced. At the same time, several seemingly small adjustments resulted not only in the abolition of earnings-related supplements but also in a substantial erosion of the traditional logic of insurance. Since 1997, successive Labour Governments refrained from making further adjustments to the second level of conditionality, i.e. they left eligibility criteria unchanged while the first and, particularly, the third level of conditionality moved to centre stage. Initially, more 'positive' forms of activation were limited to providing increased help with job search, intensive counselling and employment guidance for the unemployed; but latterly, under the Coalition Governments, and when unemployment and sanctions were both at their peak, the sanctions regime was tightened. At the same time, there was a blurring of the boundaries between unemployment and other social risks as conduct conditionality was extended to other groups, such as the disabled and single-parent families that had formerly been beyond its reach. Clasen and Clegg conclude that developments in the UK can be understood as a gradual progression down through the levers of conditionality, from adjustments at the primary level, accompanied and gradually superseded by successive initiatives that have tightened conditionality at the secondary level, before finally concentrating on tertiary conditions (through an increased emphasis on activation). This activation logic has seen a small move back up the levels of conditionality, with a partial reversal of earlier changes to primary-level criteria. They then proceed to compare this with the different patterns of development in Germany, France and Denmark.

It is clear from this account that conditionality, in the sense of attaching activation conditions to the receipt of benefits, has become more widespread in the UK. After being applied first to the unemployed, it was then applied to the long-term sick and disabled and to lone parents. As shown in Chapter 4, for five years from 2009 to 2013, increased numbers of sanctions were imposed, and more claimants were subjected to them. Thus, the 'sanctions net' became wider and deeper.

## RETHINKING THE BALANCE BETWEEN RIGHTS AND RESPONSIBILITIES

### *The Emphasis on Rights*

The eminent British sociologist T.H. Marshall defined citizenship as a status granted to everyone who is a full member of a political community, and argued that it referred to the rights and duties they have in common.[5] He focused on rights, to which citizens are entitled, rather than duties to contribute to society, and argued that citizenship consists of three clusters of rights: civil rights, political rights and social rights.

- **Civil rights** refer to rights which are necessary for individual freedom, the right to own property and make valid contracts, the right to freedom of thought and speech, and the right to justice.
- **Political rights** refer to the right to participate in the exercise of power, both as a voter and as a candidate, and in this way to hold government to account.
- **Social rights** refer to the rights to social security, health care, education, housing and social care, and to rights in relation to employment.

According to Marshall, a welfare state is a state in which citizens enjoy extensive civil rights, extensive political rights and extensive social rights. Each of these clusters of rights is associated with a different set of institutions: civil rights are associated with the legal system, i.e. with lawyers and the courts, political rights with the political system, i.e. with elections and parliaments, and social rights with the welfare system, i.e. with a range of welfare institutions.

---

[5]    Marshall (1963: Chapter 4).

Marshall noted that citizenship as such did not exist in feudal society. The formative period in Britain for civil rights was the eighteenth century, for political rights it was the nineteenth century, and for social rights it was the twentieth century, although these periods overlap to some degree. Thus, the process was sequential—civil rights came first, political rights next and social rights last—and evolutionary—and the welfare state was the culmination of this evolutionary process.

Marshall was not very explicit about the mechanisms that drove this sequential and evolutionary process. However, they would seem to involve a combination of system needs and social action, i.e. a mixture of structure and agency.[6] The emergence of capitalism gave rise to new social classes who demanded and successfully obtained a set of civil rights that were necessary for its' further development. Having obtained these civil rights, newly emergent social classes made use of them, particularly the rights to freedom of speech and freedom of assembly, to demand and obtain greater political rights. Newly enfranchised sections of the population then demanded and obtained enhancements to their social rights. Marshall's argument is a bottom-up one. Ultimately, according to him, capitalism necessarily evolves into the welfare state that, far from undermining capitalism, strengthens and legitimates it.

Although Marshall's account has been very influential, particularly in Britain, it has also come in for a great deal of criticism. Michael Mann has put forward four criticisms of Marshall's thesis.[7] He argued that it was entirely about Britain and that other countries did not fit the British model. He contended that citizenship is not necessarily built up in the sequence Marshall describes and that capitalism does not necessarily lead to the welfare state. He criticised the bottom-up emphasis in Marshall's account and argued that, since the ruling classes possess most power, they play a far more important role than Marshall was prepared to acknowledge. Finally, he argued that Marshall failed to appreciate that the effects of war explain why some sets of social arrangements have prevailed at the expense of others.

According to Mann, the comparative historical analysis of industrial societies reveals five viable strategies for what he calls the 'institutionalisation of class conflict' rather than the single strategy described by Marshall.

---

[6] Contemporary sociology has generally aimed toward a reconciliation of the concepts of structure and agency. See, for example, Giddens (1984) and Bourdieu (1990).

[7] Mann (1987).

**Table 5.1**   Different patterns of citizenship rights

| Model | Examples | Civil rights | Political rights | Social rights |
|---|---|---|---|---|
| Liberal | USA, Switzerland | Strong | Strong | Weak |
| Reformist (social democratic) | Scandinavia, other Western European countries | Strong | Strong | Strong |
| Authoritarian monarchist | Imperial Germany, Russia and Japan | Strong | Weak | Weak |
| Fascist | Nazi Germany, Fascist Italy and Fascist Spain | Weak | Weak | Strong |
| Authoritarian socialist | Soviet Union | Weak | Weak | Strong |

Mann calls these the liberal, the reformist, the authoritarian monarchist, the fascist and the 'authoritarian socialist' strategies. The different patterns of citizenship rights associated with each of the five strategic outcomes are set out in Table 5.1.

It will be noted that Table 5.1 makes no reference to the UK and it is unclear which model Mann thinks it exemplifies. When Marshall wrote 'Citizenship and Social Class' in 1949, in the hey-day of the post-war Labour Government, he clearly thought it exemplified the reformist (social democratic) model. However, in light of subsequent developments, the consensus of opinion is that this is no longer the case and that it now exemplifies the liberal model, characterised by strong civil and political rights and weak economic and social rights.[8]

One limitation of Mann's approach is that the categories 'weak' and 'strong' are extremely crude and it would obviously be better if more sophisticated measures of the extent of citizenship rights in different countries were available. Another limitation is its static nature and the fact that it does not take account of the fact that patterns of citizenship rights in different countries, for example the UK, can change over time. However, his analysis does make it clear that, as far as citizenship rights are concerned, strong civil rights do not necessarily lead to strong social rights and strong social rights are not necessarily preceded by strong civil rights. It is also clear that there is considerable variation in the extent of civil, political and social rights in different countries and that each combination is associated with a different conception of citizenship.

[8]   See, most famously, Esping-Andersen (1990). It is significant that this work focuses on social security.

The British political philosopher W.B. Gallie argued that there is a class of political concepts which can be defined in relatively uncontentious ways but are open to a range of interpretations. He referred to them as 'essentially contested concepts'.[9] Following Marshall, citizenship has been defined in terms of the rights and duties that those who are full members of a political community have in common as citizens. However, this leaves open the nature of the rights and duties in question, the balance between them and the identity of the political community, which may be an independent state but may equally be something more extensive, e.g. the international community, or something more limited, e.g. a devolved entity within the state. The different patterns of civil, political and social rights associated with different types of state that were set out in Table 5.1 suggest that citizenship is such a concept. If this is the case, it follows that there is no single model of citizenship which applies 'across the board' and that different models coexist with each other.

In the days of the 'cold war', there was an ongoing conflict between the USA (and its supporters) and the Soviet Union (and its followers) over whether the capitalist system (in its American form) or the communist system (in its Russian form) took rights more seriously. With the collapse of the Soviet Union and the end of the Cold War, these arguments are now more muted. However, there is still an argument between exponents of free market capitalism, who seek to defend a conception of citizenship based exclusively on strong civil and political rights, and exponents of welfare capitalism, who seek to defend a conception of citizenship that combines a strong commitment to social rights with a strong commitment to civil and political rights. The IMF and the World Bank, which have sought to promote deregulation and the liberalisation of markets, privatisation and the downsizing of governments, are generally thought to be in the first camp while the European Union, which has sought to promote the European Social Model, is generally placed in the second camp. These two positions are set out in Table 5.2.

Although Marshall defined citizenship in terms of the rights and duties granted to everyone who is a full member of a political community, his discussion of citizenship book focused on rights, i.e. on the claims that individuals can make on other individuals, on institutions and on the state, and had little to say about duties or responsibilities, i.e. about the what individuals owe to other individuals, institutions and society.

[9] Gallie (1955–1956).

**Table 5.2** Competing contemporary conceptions of citizenship rights

| System | Exemplar | Civil rights | Political rights | Social rights |
|---|---|---|---|---|
| Liberal capitalism | USA | Strong | Strong | Weak |
| Welfare capitalism | EU | Strong | Strong | Strong |

Some critics, on the communitarian left (who value solidarity and mutuality) as well as on the libertarian or neo-conservative right (who value autonomy and freedom), have argued that a one-sided emphasis on rights can be corrosive of the fabric of society and that it has contributed to many of the problems faced by Western societies. According to Amitai Etzioni,[10] the mismatch between rights and responsibilities has led to widespread social malaise characterised by people claiming rights for themselves and leaving the exercise of responsibilities to others. Communitarians point out that people live unhealthy lives but expect doctors and other health care providers to treat them when they get ill, and that parents do not nurture their children or encourage their intellectual development but expect teachers to educate them. They point out that, while some parents abuse and neglect their children, society expects social workers to prevent the children from coming to any harm. The communitarian strategy for dealing with these problems has several strands and involves (i) a moratorium on the granting of new rights; (ii) re-establishing the link between rights and responsibilities, (iii) recognising that some responsibilities, e.g. for improving the environment, do not entail rights; and (iv) adjusting some rights to changed circumstances. An example of the second strand was the introduction of conditionality in social security, i.e. requiring those who were unemployed to undertake suitable training, actively look for work and apply for available jobs.

## CONCLUSION: RECALIBRATING THE BALANCE BETWEEN RIGHTS AND RESPONSIBILITIES

Underpinning the changes described in Chapters 3 and 4 above was a shift in the way government understood the relationship between the citizen and the state. In its Welfare Reform Green Paper,[11] published

[10] Etzioni (1995).
[11] Department of Social Security (1998).

in 1998, the Labour Government proposed 'a new contract for welfare between the citizen and the state with rights matched by responsibilities' making it clear that 'it is the responsibility of the government to provide positive help... [and] the responsibility of the claimant to take it up'. New rights were to be granted to claimants in return for the acceptance of new responsibilities. The new rights included the right to expect government to guarantee the availability of good quality job-search advice, training opportunities and employment (in a normal, unsubsidised job or in a job subsidised by the state). The new responsibilities involved an obligation to take full advantage of these opportunities. A 'hand-up' rather than a 'hand-out' became the new mantra[12] and work rather than benefits became the main route to 'social security'. However, there was no mention in the new contract of the penalties that would be imposed, in the form of benefit sanctions, on those who failed to meet their responsibilities. Thus, there was no suggestion that they might be denied their civil rights, such as the right to due process, or their political rights, such as the right to the respect owed to others who are full members of the political community. The question that needs to be asked is whether, in light of the significant increase in benefit conditions and benefit sanctions in the last 20 years, the balance between rights and responsibilities has become too one sided.

## REFERENCES

Bourdieu, P. (1990). *The Logic of Practice*. Cambridge: Polity Press.

Clasen, J., & Clegg, D. (2007). Levels and Levers of Conditionality: Measuring Change within Welfare States. In J. Clasen & N. A. Siegal (Eds.), *Investigating Welfare State Change. The 'Dependent Variable Problem' in Comparative Analysis* (pp. 166–197). Cheltenham: Edward Elgar.

Department of Social Security. (1998). *New Ambitions for Our Country: New Contract for Welfare*, Cm. 3805. London: HMSO.

Esping-Andersen, G. (1990). *The Three Worlds of Welfare Capitalism*. Cambridge: Polity Press.

Etzioni, A. (1995). *The Spirit of Community*. London: Fontana.

Gallie, W. B. (1955–1956). Essentially Contested Concepts. *Proceedings of the Aristotelian Society*, 56, 167–198. Reprinted as Chapter 8 in Gallie, W. B. (1964). *Philosophy and the Historical Understanding*. London: Chatto and Windus.

---

[12] It has become the slogan of the street newspaper *The Big Issue*, founded in 1991.

Giddens, A. (1984). *The Constitution of Society*. Cambridge: Polity Press.

Knotz, C., & Nelson. M. (2013, September 5–7). *Quantifying Conditionality: A New Database on Conditions and Sanctions for Unemployment Benefit Claimants*. Paper prepared for the ESPAnet Conference, Poznan. Available at https://ssrn.com/abstract=2328253 or http://dx.doi.org/10.2189/ssrn.2328253.

Langenbucher, K. (2015). *How Demanding are Eligibility Criteria for Unemployment Benefits—Quantitative Indicators for OECD and EU Countries* (OECD Social, Employment and Migration Papers, No. 166).

Mann, M. (1987). Ruling Class Strategies and Citizenship. *Sociology, 21*(3), 339–354.

Marshall, T. H. (1963). Citizenship and Social Class. In *Sociology at the Crossroads* (Chapter 4). London: Routledge.

Watts, B., Fitzpatrick, S., Bramley, G., & Watkins, D. (2014). *Welfare Sanctions and Conditionality in the UK*. York: Joseph Rowntree Foundation.

CHAPTER 6

# The Impact and Effectiveness of Benefit Sanctions

Although the main stated goal of conditionality, i.e. of eligibility and entitlement conditions and benefit sanctions, within the social security system is to influence claimants' behaviour by incentivising them to actively seek work and to move off benefits into employment, there is little systematic evidence on whether conditionality has been successful in the UK. However, there have been two recent studies, a statistical analysis of two aggregate data sets and an analysis of Work Programme data held by the Department for Work and Pensions (DWP) by the National Audit office, and the chapter considers these two studies in some detail. It also looks at evidence of the impact of sanctions on claimants' well-being and at the ways in which benefit sanctions produce real hardship and can lead to destitution. Finally, it looks at the operation of the DWP's hardship payment scheme and asks whether hardship payments provide a reasonable degree of protection against financial hardship.

## THE LOGIC OF CONDITIONALITY

The logic underlying the emphasis placed on conditionality in the JSA (Jobseeker's allowance), ESA (Employment and Support Allowance) and UC schemes is one in which the government undertakes to help people on benefit to find a job as long as they do what is expected of them (in terms of doing enough to find work, not turning down jobs offered to

© The Author(s) 2018
M. Adler, *Cruel, Inhuman or Degrading Treatment?*, Palgrave
Socio-Legal Studies, https://doi.org/10.1007/978-3-319-90356-9_6

them and turning upkeeping for appointments) and, if they do not do what is expected of them, they will be sanctioned, that is their benefit will be stopped.[1] Although there is a notional balance between rights (to benefit) and responsibilities (to look for work), this balance is a very lop-sided one.[2] The pendulum has swung from one extreme to the other, from what some people regarded as an over-emphasis on rights to what many people now argue is an over-emphasis on responsibilities. This is illustrated by the fact that, an estimated 50,000 JSA sanctions and 6,200 ESA sanctions were overturned in 2015 following a review, a reconsideration or an appeal.[3] This comprises a total of 56,200 cases in which the claimant's payments will have been erroneously stopped for weeks or months only to be refunded later, i.e. a total of 56,200 cases in which the claimant was penalised in error. If one adds to this number the presumably larger number of claimants who were sanctioned but should not have been but who, for one reason or another, did not challenge the decision, the amount of unnecessary suffering imposed by the system is quite staggering.

## THE IMPACT OF SANCTIONS ON RETURN TO WORK

Seven years ago, based on a systematic review of international evidence, Griggs and Evans concluded that 'sanctions for employment-related conditions strongly reduce benefit use and raise exits from benefit, but have generally unfavourable effects on longer-term outcomes (such as employment and earnings) and spill-over effects (e.g. on crime rates). In other words, although benefit sanctions get claimants off benefit, they do not get them into work.[4]

It is a matter of considerable disappointment, both for supporters of conditionality, who believe that the imposition of job search requirements and benefit sanctions are effective means of preventing abuse and getting those on benefit back into work, and for its critics, who believe that they are ineffective and cause considerable suffering, that the UK Government has not undertaken any research that would enable these

[1]   See Watts et al. (2014: 7).
[2]   For a compelling account of the ways in which restrictive 'workfare' measures have been combined with expansive 'prison fare' to produce an extremely punitive approach to poverty management in the USA, see Wacquant (2009).
[3]   See Chapter 7 below.
[4]   Griggs and Evans (2010).

concerns to be addressed. It has recently been roundly criticised for this in a report by the National Audit Office (NAO).[5]

In evidence to the NAO, the DWP cited 13 studies of the impact of sanctions carried out in Denmark, Germany, Great Britain, the Netherlands, Sweden, Switzerland, and the USA.[6] However, while these studies show that sanctions do persuade some people to take up work, they also demonstrate that they encourage others to 'drop out', i.e. to stop claiming without taking up work. Some sanctioned claimants undoubtedly experience hardship, becoming homeless, engaging in street begging or in crime, while others rely on income and support from friends and family.

Evidence about the effectiveness of sanctions is available from an independent study of two aggregate data sets carried out recently by a team of researchers from Oxford.[7] This study revealed that the introduction of the more severe sanctions regime in 2012 led to a substantial increase in the number of people leaving benefit.[8] Most of those who left benefit did not move into employment but rather into 'unknown destinations', i.e. to destinations other than employment or to a further period on benefit. Thus, for each 100 adverse sanction decisions in the previous three months, only 7.4 claimants moved off benefit and into employment whereas 35.9 claimants moved off benefit into destinations unrelated to employment. It is reasonable to assume that they 'dropped out'. The remainder returned to benefit but many of those who were sanctioned ended up staying with relatives or friends or sleeping rough. These results should be treated with some caution because relationships between aggregates do not necessarily hold at the individual level.[9]

To see how the DWP could use its data, the NAO analysed Work Programme data from 2014 to see how receiving a sanction affected JSA and ESA claimants' employment, earnings and time off benefits without work.

---

[5]  In 2015, DWP advised Work Programme providers not to participate in focus groups for the £2 million, ESRC-funded Welfare Conditionality Project. See Comptroller and Auditor General (2016: para 3.8).

[6]  Comptroller and Auditor General (2016: Fig. 21).

[7]  The Department for Work and Pensions (DWP) Sanctions Dataset (Stat-Xplore) and the Office of National Statistics (ONS) Labour Market Statistics (Nomis).

[8]  Loopstra et al. (2015).

[9]  Assuming that aggregate relationships apply at the individual level is a common statistical error known as the 'ecological fallacy'.

It concluded that, for JSA claimants, 'sanctions had a large and significant impact on claimants who were sanctioned—they were as likely to find work as they were to stop working but, for ESA claimants, they had much less effect'.[10] The key findings, which are elaborated in a technical report, are as follows[11]:

- For those formerly in receipt of JSA, sanctions *increased* the probability of being in employment in later months, *reduced* the number of days claiming benefits, *increased* the number of days in employment, and *increased* the number of days neither in employment not claiming benefit.
- For those formerly in receipt of ESA, sanctions *reduced* the probability of being in employment in later months, *increased* the number of days claiming benefits and not working, and *increased* the number of days neither in employment not claiming benefit.

Most of the results were statistically significant.[12] They show that sanctions were successful in getting some unspecified number of JSA claimants into low-paid work but were not similarly successful with ESA claimants and that, at the same time, JSA and ESA claimants were more likely to end up neither in work not on benefit, i.e. dropping out. The results from the two studies are not comparable because, unlike the Oxford study, the NAO study did not generate numerical estimates.

Although the threat of sanctions is clearly instrumental in persuading some claimants to participate in work programmes and to step up their job-search activities, both these studies indicate that the imposition of sanctions propels many claimants away from the benefit system and from 'mainstream' institutions, and that it distances them from work as well as from benefits. Even if sanctions, or the threat of sanctions, are effective in persuading some people to move from benefits into work, it is important to ask whether these gains outweigh the many documented costs of sanctions in terms of the hardship they cause. No such an assessment has ever been made by the DWP.

It is also important to ask why sanctions do not work as effectively as the proponents of conditionality believed they would. One explanation

---

[10] Comptroller and Auditor General (2016: paras 3.9, 3.10).
[11] National Audit Office (2016: para 43).
[12] National Audit Office (2016: paras 34, 36).

is that they are based on the paradigm of neo-classical micro-economic theory, which asserts that human conduct is the outcome of a rational choice between various alternatives in which people seek to maximise their self-interest. Critics have called this theory of self-interest into question, arguing that, in practice, most people do not seek to maximise their self-interest. According to neo-classical theory, the imposition of benefit sanctions, which result in the withdrawal of benefits from job-seekers and others who are out of work, should shift the balance towards more actively looking for and ultimately finding remunerative employment.

## The Impact of Sanctions on Claimants' Well-Being

There is a mounting body of evidence that vulnerable people, for example homeless people, those with learning disabilities and immigrants with a limited understanding of English, are more likely to be sanctioned than others. A joint analysis of DWP statistics by *The Independent* and the mental health charity *Mind*[13] found that 19,259 people with mental health conditions received a benefit sanction in 2014–2015 compared to just 2,507 in 2011–2012—a massive increase over a period in which the number of sanctions that were imposed actually declined.[14] However, the Government rejected a call to investigate whether benefit sanctions are damaging to mental health. Thus, the available evidence suggests that benefit sanctions are not only targeted at the poorest in society but disproportionately affect the most disadvantaged of poor people.

Further, there is considerable evidence that many of those who are subject to benefit sanctions suffer considerable hardship, that sanctions can have a detrimental effect on health and well-being, and that many of those who are sanctioned end up homeless,[15] engage in street begging, use food banks and resort to crime. The widespread and chronic hardship that results from the imposition of benefit sanctions suggests that they are excessive and disproportionate.

---

[13] See Stone (2015).

[14] There were 741,000 JSA and ESA sanctions in 2014 and 383,000 in 2015 compared to 743,000 in 2011 and 918,000 in 2012. See Table 4.2 above.

[15] This is because the Jobcentre contacts the Council, which then stops the payment of housing benefit until the claimant provides proof of his/her reduced income (or that he/she no longer have any income) and his/her housing benefit is reassessed. Doing nothing will mean that the claimant ends up with rent (and Council Tax) arrears and may end up homeless.

Although there is no robust data tracing the extent to which the imposition of sanctions gives rise to hardship, there is a good deal of anecdotal evidence. A recent study of destitution in the UK,[16] defined people as destitute *either* if they or their children lacked two or more of six essentials in the previous month, because they could not afford them *or* because their income was so extremely low that they were unable to purchase these essentials themselves. 40% of the estimated total of 1,250,000 destitute people were destitute on both criteria, 49% on the first criterion only, i.e. they could not afford to purchase two or more of the essential items although their incomes were above the 'extremely low' standard, and 12% on the second criterion only, i.e. they had been able to purchase the essential items although their incomes were below the 'extremely low' standard.

Although it is conventional to think of social security as a social institution that prevents or ameliorates destitution, and it probably is for most people most of the time, some of the procedures it adopts, such as delays in the processing of benefit claims and the imposition of benefit sanctions, can give rise to destitution. Some categories of people, for example asylum seekers and undocumented migrants, are not able to claim social security while, among those who can claim, delays in processing claims and sanctions that penalise claimants for failing to meet the increasingly onerous requirements that are associated with the receipt of social security benefits, can result in destitution.

Benefit delays were the most frequently reported benefit problem reported in the JRF study, affecting 40% of all destitute service users in the survey of voluntary sector crisis centres.[17] Interviewees waiting for JSA payments to start experienced delays of up to six weeks, which presented serious problems for those moving in and out of casual or short-term work. Some interviewees claimed that repeated administrative failures in processing their claims had led to serious delays and caused considerable hardship.

Benefit sanctions were reported by 30% of destitute service users. As noted above, they were disproportionately applied to vulnerable claimants. Although the threat of being sanctioned probably does persuade some claimants to step up their job-search activities, the Oxford study's findings indicate that the main effect of imposing sanctions was to eject claimants undertaken by from the benefits system and to distance them

---

[16] Fitzpatrick et al. (2016).

[17] Fitzpatrick et al. (2016: 31–32).

from the world of work.[18] As noted above, many of them end up homeless, begging on the street, using food banks and resorting to crime.

## Hardship Payments

Being sanctioned is not necessarily the end of the line. Once sanctioned, claimants can apply for hardship payments. To get these, they are required to prove that they are at risk of financial hardship. Decisions about hardship payments are made by DWP decision-makers and, in determining whether a claimant is eligible for hardship payments, the decision-maker should, among other things, look at whether there is a substantial risk that the claimant will not be able to buy essential items, including food, clothing, heating and accommodation.

If claimants are eligible for hardship payments, unless they are identified as being in a vulnerable group—which, until April 2017, did not include those who were homeless or mentally ill—typically received 60% of their personal allowance from the 15th day of the sanction period. If they were deemed to be in a vulnerable group, they could apply immediately and receive 80% of their personal entitlement. Unfortunately, sanctioned claimants are often not told about hardship payments and the DWP has itself has acknowledged that that the two-week wait will often damage the claimant's health.[19]

The criteria for 'hardship' are specific to the sanctions regime and can be very harsh—for example, a person with cash in hand equal to their 'applicable amount'[20] will be refused even if the money is owed to a pay day lender. If someone gets a hardship payment, this means, in effect, that they have used up all their resources and exhausted all possibility of obtaining help from their family or their friends.

Until recently, no statistics on hardship payments have been available. However, in November 2015, the DWP published monthly statistics on JSA and ESA hardship payment applications and awards covering the period April 2012 to June 2015. The most striking feature of the time-series data in Fig. 6.1 is the substantial increase in the number of hardship payments immediately after the introduction of the more severe

---

[18] Loopstra et al. (2015).

[19] This is acknowledged at para. 35099 in the DWP Decision Makers' Guide.

[20] The amount of money a person is expected to live off. It comprises a personal allowance, premiums for extra needs, and allowable housing costs for home owners.

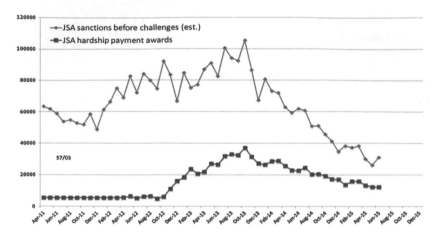

**Fig. 6.1** JSA sanctions (before challenges) and hardship payment awards, 2011–2015 (*Source* Webster, David (2015) JSA and ESA hardship applications and awards. April 2012 to June 2015. Early Briefing, Fig. 1, available at http://cpag.org.uk/david-webster)

sanctions regime in October 2012. Since then the gap between the number of sanctions and the number of hardship awards has continued to narrow.

Before the October 2012 changes, JSA hardship awards were running at less than 10% of the number of sanctions imposed. However, they then rose steeply, to 30% in February 2013, and, after that, they rose further, to over 40% in October 2014. This can be seen in Fig. 6.2.

However, it is important to stress that these ratios give an overly optimistic impression of the extent to which hardship payments mitigate the effects of sanctions. Hardship payments are 'one-off' payments and, if someone applies for a second hardship payment, that is recorded as a second payment. Under JSA and ESA, a successful application for a hardship payment ensures that it continues to be paid for the whole of the sanction period. However, under UC, claimants have to reapply for hardship payments every month. Thus, the number of people who are helped by hardship payments is less than the number of payments made. Sanctions, on the other hand, are continuing penalties that apply for periods of four weeks, 13 weeks or three years.

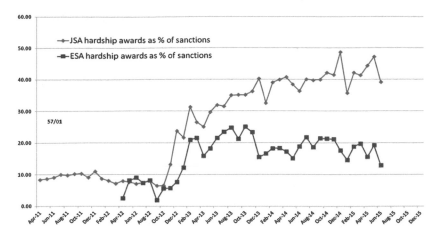

**Fig. 6.2** Hardship payment awards as a percentage of JSA and ESA sanctions (before challenges), 2001–2015 (*Source* Webster, David (2015) *JSA and ESA hardship applications and awards. April 2012 to June 2015. Early Briefing*, Fig. 2, available at http://cpag.org.uk/david-webster)

Since August 2012, most sanctions that ended had lasted for four weeks (or less) and relatively few had lasted for more than 13 weeks. However, about one third of those who received a benefit sanction received no benefit for more than four weeks. The figures for JSA, ESA and UC are set out in Table 6.1 and it can be seen that sanctions for UC claimants last considerably longer than sanctions for JSA and ESA claimants. The sanctions regime appears to have become stricter rather than more lenient.

Hardship payments clearly provide some compensation for the loss of benefit. However, what, at first sight, looks like a reasonable degree of protection turns out, on closer inspection, to be less than adequate. As with any discretionary benefit, the complicated application process and lack of information given to claimants mean that many claimants never apply for the 'hardship payments', which they would probably receive if they were to apply; even when an application is made, most claimants have to wait 15 days before they can apply and there are often delays in payment. That said, most of those who do apply for hardship payments receive them: just under 90% of sanctioned JSA claimants who apply are successful.

**Table 6.1**   Duration of sanctions for JSA, ESA and UC, 2012/2015–2017

| | JSA[a] | | ESA[b] | | UC[c] | |
|---|---|---|---|---|---|---|
| | Number | % | Number | % | Number | % |
| 4 weeks (or less) | 279,900 | 63 | 37,100 | 57 | 75,200 | 50 |
| 5–13 weeks | 139,600 | 32 | 16,700 | 26 | 60,400 | 40 |
| 14–26 weeks | 16,700 | 4 | 6200 | 10 | 11,000 | 7 |
| 27 weeks and over | 5400 | 1 | 5400 | 8 | 2700 | 2 |

[a]October 2012–March 2017
[b]October 2012–March 2017
[c]October 2015–March 2017
*Source* Department for Work and Pensions (2017) *Benefit Sanctions Statistics*, June, available at https://www.gov.uk/government/uploads/system/uploads/attachment_data/file/661218/benefit-sanctions-statistics-to-june-2017.pdf

Sanctioned ESA claimants have not, until recently, been as badly off as sanctioned JSA claimants since they retained the 'work related activity component' of their benefit. However, this provision was abolished in April 2017. They are also, in general, a less disadvantaged group than JSA claimants, in that long-term sickness and disability are less concentrated among economically disadvantaged people than is unemployment. These factors probably explain why, although ESA hardship awards rose sharply when sanctions were increased in October 2012, the proportion of sanctioned ESA claimants receiving hardship payments has never been as high as the proportion of sanctioned JSA claimants. They rose from under 10% during 2012 to around 20%, with the proportion declining slightly over the period since 2013.

Altogether, 749,900 JSA and 18,650 ESA hardship payments were awarded over the period covered by these statistics, a total of 768,550 payments. Some of them will have been repeat awards to the same people, but on the other hand these figures do not include people who should have applied but did not. This may seem like a reasonable degree of protection but, when compared to the 3,154,432 JSA sanctions and 100,627 ESA sanctions, i.e. to the total of 3,255,059 sanctions that were imposed and, more to the point, to the duration of the sanctions, the degree of protection they provided was quite limited.

## CLAIMANTS' EXPERIENCE OF HARDSHIP PAYMENTS

The two reports that were used to illustrate the circumstances that gave rise to sanctions cited in Chapter 4[21] reveal that a significant number of sanctioned claimants reported that they were not aware of, and were not told about, hardship payments. Below is a selection of cases in which this is alleged to have been the case.

> Clare (24) had been moved to JSA from ESA six months previously, but still suffered from depression, anxiety, alcoholism and asthma. She was unaware that she had been sanctioned until the benefit did not go into her account and she enquired at the Job Centre. She was not advised about hardship payments and so received no money at all for six weeks. (SUWN Case 17)

> Lynn (52) had been sanctioned twice. She was sanctioned for four weeks for not making enough job applications and because her job-search notes were too short. Two years later, she was sanctioned for twelve weeks for a missed appointment at Triage, but claims she had not received an appointment letter ... On both occasions, she had to be referred to a food bank. (SUWN Case 27)

> Gav (34) was sanctioned for six weeks over Christmas and New Year 2012-13 as a result of being in hospital for eight weeks for an operation on his feet due to bad circulation. (His feet were black and he was on crutches; he also suffers from epilepsy.) Gav was informed that he was at fault for missing his appointment. He had asked if financial help was available, but had received nothing. (SUWN Case 68)

Some of those who applied for hardship payments were ineligible and others were turned down.

> Gary (39) had twice been sanctioned via Triage. The first sanction was for four weeks for a missed appointment. However, he had previously informed Triage [the local Work Programme provider] and the Job Centre that he was unavailable on that date as he had a meeting to discuss funding for his volunteer position at the Deaf Hub—which could potentially have led to a full-time job. Although he was aware of the existence of hardship payments, he was told he was not eligible to receive anything. (SUWN Case 58)

[21] Scottish Unemployed Workers' Network (2014) and Citizens Advice Scotland (2012).

Hardship payments are discretionary, and the rates vary, as the cases reported below show. According to those who were interviewed, there appeared to be three bands: £40–45 per fortnight, £60–65 per fortnight and £80–85 per fortnight (at 2014 rates)[22]—all of them quite insufficient to live off. They were not made for the first two weeks unless the claimant was classed as 'vulnerable' and had no other means of support.

## CONCLUSION: THE IMPACT OF BENEFIT SANCTIONS ON RETURN TO WORK AND CLAIMANTS' WELL-BEING

It is often said that ignorance is bliss. By not conducting any research or analysing the statistics that are clearly available as a routine bi-product of administration, the DWP could claim not to know what the impact of benefit sanctions is. However, it is quite extraordinary, perhaps even negligent, of the DWP to have been so indifferent to the effectiveness of the policies it has pursued or their impact on claimants. The available evidence reviewed in this chapter makes it clear that benefit sanctions are not all that effective, in that although some JSA claimants who are sanctioned subsequently enter employment, this is not the case for ESA claimants, and that, for both JSA and ESA claimants, many of those who are sanctioned end up neither on benefit nor in work, i.e. dropping out of the system. At the same time, it is clear is that sanctions impose a great deal of suffering on those who are subject to them. Everyone who has looked at benefit sanctions knows this but those who could have done something about it have chosen not to do so.

Although it is conventional to think of social security as a social institution that prevents or ameliorates destitution, it does not always do so. This is the case with benefit sanctions and the recent Joseph Rowntree Foundation study, *Destitution in the UK*, found that 30% of those who were destitute reported that they had been subject to benefit sanctions. Although the DWP does operate a hardship payment scheme, and some 40% of sanctioned claimants receive one or more hardship awards, an

---

[22] Gary (39) reported receiving £40 after two weeks with no money (SUWP Case 22), Isobel (52) said she received £40 and Rick said he received £42 (SUWP Case 36); Willie claimed he received £68 (SUWP Case 44), Keith (20) reported receiving £60 (SUWP Case 47), Simon (20) £57 (SUWL Case 70); Kevin said he had received £87 (SUWP Case 38), Gordon reported receiving £84 (SUWP Case 39); while Robbie (46) said he had received £86 (SUWP Case 72).

analysis of the published statistics, and the accounts of claimants' experiences presented in this chapter indicate that the degree of protection they provide is very limited indeed.

## REFERENCES

Citizens Advice Scotland. (2012). *Voices from the Frontline: JSA Sanctions.* Edinburgh. Available at https://www.cas.org.uk/publications/voices-frontline-jsa-sanctions.

Comptroller and Auditor General. (2016). *Benefit Sanctions,* HC 628, Session 2016–17. London: National Audit Office. Available at https://www.nao.org.uk/wp-content/uploads/2016/11/Benefit-sanctions.pdf.

Fitzpatrick, S., Bramley, G., Sosenko, F., Blenkinsopp, J., Johnsen, S., Littlewood, M., Netto, G., & Watts, B. (2016). *Destitution in the UK.* York: Joseph Rowntree Foundation. Available at https://www.jrf.org.uk/report/destitution-uk.

Griggs, J., & Evans, M. (2010). *Sanctions within Conditional Benefit Systems: A Review of Evidence.* York: Joseph Rowntree Foundantion.

Loopstra, R., Reeves, A., McKee, M., & Suckler, D. (2015). *Do Punitive Approaches to Unemployment Benefit Recipients Increase Welfare Exit and Unemployment: A Cross-Area Analysis of UK Sanctioning Reforms* (Sociology Working Paper 2015–01), Department of Sociology, University of Oxford. Available at http://www.sociology.ox.ac.uk/working-papers/do-punitive-approaches-to-unemployment-benefit-recipients-increase-welfare-exit-and-employment-a-cross-area-analysis-of-uk-sanctioning-reforms.html.

National Audit Office. (2016, November 17). *Benefit Sanctions: Detailed Methodology.* London: National Audit Office. Available at https://www.nao.org.uk/wp-content/uploads/2016/11/Benefit-sanctions-detailedmethodology.pdf.

Scottish Unemployed Workers' Network. (2014, December). *Sanctioned Voices: A Report on the Impact of the DWP Sanctions Regime as Implemented in Dundee Job Centre, Compiled by Volunteers for the Scottish Unemployed Workers' Network.* Available at https://suwn.files.wordpress.com/2015/12/sanctioned_voices.pdf.

Stone, J. (2015, November 12). Benefit Sanctions Against People with Mental Health Problems up by 600 per cent. *The Independent.* Available at http://www.independent.co.uk/news/uk/politics/benefit-sanctions-against-people-with-mental-health-problems-up-by-600-per-cent-a6731971.html.

Wacquant, L. (2009). *Punishing the Poor: The Neoliberal Government of Social Insecurity.* Durham, NC and London: Duke University Press.

Watts, B., Fitzpatrick, S., Bramley, G., & Watkins, D. (2014). *Welfare Sanctions and Conditionality in the UK.* York: Joseph Rowntree Foundation.

Webster, D. (2015a, February 18). *Briefing: The DWP's JSA/ESA Sanctions Statistics Release.* Available at http://www.cpag.org/david-webster.

Webster, D. (2015b, May 13). *Briefing: The DWP's JSA/ESA Sanctions Statistics Release.* Available at http://www.cpag.org/david-webster.

# CHAPTER 7

# Benefit Sanctions and Administrative Justice

The terms *civil justice* and *criminal justice* are familiar and reasonably well understood in the UK. However, this is not the case with the term *administrative justice*, which is still shrouded in obscurity. Some people use the term to describe the principles of administrative law formulated by the superior courts (and the top tiers of other redress mechanisms) in the small number of cases that come before them. Other people use the term to refer to the justice found in the myriad of routine administrative decisions taken by central and local government departments. This chapter adopts a hybrid approach and uses the term to describe the justice encountered in the end-to-end process that starts with first-instance administrative decisions and ends with cases taken on appeal to the highest courts. It highlights one approach to administrative justice, associated with the American public lawyer Jerry Mashaw, which asserts that it can be understood in terms of trade-offs between different normative models of decision making that compete for ascendancy and between the individuals and groups associated with them. It considers the impact of five organisational changes considered in Chapters 3 and 4, all of which have implications for the trade-offs that are achieved, especially the introduction of internal review, known as Mandatory Reconsideration (MR), and the resulting decline in the number of appeals. By way of conclusion, the chapter considers the limited impact of law in protecting those who are subject to benefit sanctions.

© The Author(s) 2018
M. Adler, *Cruel, Inhuman or Degrading Treatment?*, Palgrave
Socio-Legal Studies, https://doi.org/10.1007/978-3-319-90356-9_7

## TREATING PEOPLE FAIRLY[1]

A distinction is often made between *procedural fairness*, which can be regarded as synonymous with *procedural justice* and is concerned with 'process',[2] and *substantive justice*, which is concerned with 'outcomes'. Procedural fairness focuses on how individuals are treated while substantive justice focuses on how their circumstances change. In criminal and civil justice, procedural fairness includes the rules of evidence and procedure that govern proceedings in the criminal and civil courts, while substantive justice refers to the outcomes of criminal prosecutions and civil actions; in the case of administrative justice, procedural fairness includes the administrative rules that govern decision making by officials in government departments and other public bodies while substantive justice refers to the allocation of benefits, the delivery of services, the award of licenses, the imposition of taxes and so on. It follows that administrative justice embraces the granting of benefits and the imposition of sanctions.

It is, of course, possible to take issue with the distinction made above on the grounds that treating people fairly should itself be regarded as an outcome of the decision-making process. However, if it is an outcome, it is clearly a very different kind of outcome from most of the outcomes that procedures are established to achieve. If these are referred to as *primary outcomes*, then treating people fairly may be referred to as a *secondary outcome*. The primary outcome of criminal procedures in the criminal courts is to determine guilt and court procedures can be judged in terms of how effectively they do so, i.e. by the proportion of 'guilty people' who are acquitted and the proportion of 'innocent people' who are convicted. Likewise, the primary outcome of administrative procedures is to confer entitlements, impose obligations or regulate activities, and they may likewise be judged by the proportion of false negatives and false positives they produce. Criminal courts and administrative agencies should both aim to treat people fairly but that is not their primary purpose. Even if treating people fairly is regarded as an outcome, a distinction can be made between the just outcomes which the procedures are intended to deliver and the fairness of the ways in which the procedures deal with people. The idea of *procedural fairness* suggests that a concern with 'ensuring that everyone receives their due' can be applied to procedures and that a fair procedure

---

[1]    The discussion in this chapter draws on Adler (2010, 2012).
[2]    Richardson (1984).

is one in which individuals are treated in a manner that reflects what is due to them in light of their personal characteristics and circumstances.

There have been various attempts to specify the requirements of procedural fairness. Thus, in criminal and civil justice, reference is made to a fair trial (in the case of criminal prosecutions) and to fair proceedings (in civil matters). In a criminal prosecution, the procedural requirements reflect the rights and duties of the accused and the state. What they ought to be are matters of ongoing debate but there is wide agreement that accused persons should be entitled to know the case against them, to be legally represented, to plead not guilty and, if they do so, to be treated as innocent until found guilty. The evidence against them must stand up and the case for the prosecution must be established 'beyond reasonable doubt'. Likewise, in a civil action, where the outcome is decided 'on the balance of probabilities', there are procedural requirements, which reflect the rights and duties of the parties in dispute, which are also matters of ongoing debate.[3] To determine what the requirements of procedural fairness in administrative justice are, the concept of administrative justice needs to be unpicked.

## NORMATIVE MODELS OF ADMINISTRATIVE JUSTICE

The starting point is to identify and compare different normative models of administrative justice, defined in terms of the justice encountered in the decision-making process. According to the American public lawyer Jerry Mashaw these models are 'competitive' rather than 'mutually exclusive'.[4] This means that each normative model can and does coexist with the others but the greater is the influence of one, the lesser will be the influence of the others. In my own work, I have built on and extended Mashaw's approach and identified six models of normative justice, each of which reflects the concerns and the bargaining strengths of institutional actors who have an interest in promoting them.[5] Table 7.1 sets out the competing models of administrative justice that, I have suggested, are encountered in routine administrative decision-making today, and characterises them in terms of their mode of decision-making, their legitimating goal(s), their characteristic mode of accountability and mode of redress.

---

[3]   See, for example, Hazel Genn's 2008 Hamlyn lectures, published as Genn (2010).

[4]   Mashaw (1983: 23).

[5]   Adler (2006).

**Table 7.1**    Six normative models of administrative justice

| Model | Mode of decision-making | Legitimating goal | Mode of accountability | Mode of redress |
|---|---|---|---|---|
| Bureaucratic | Applying rules | Accuracy | Hierarchical | Administrative review |
| Professional | Applying knowledge | Public service | Interpersonal | Second opinion, complaint to a professional body or merits review |
| Juridical | Asserting rights | Legality | Independent | Appeal to a court or tribunal (public law) |
| Managerial | Managerial autonomy | Improved performance | Meeting performance targets | None, except adverse publicity or complaints that result in sanctions on management |
| Consumerist | Consumer participation | Consumer satisfaction | Consumer charters | 'voice' and/or compensation through consumer charters |
| Market | Matching supply and demand | Economic efficiency | Payment by results | 'exit' and/or court action (private law) |

Since the six normative models of administrative justice are 'competitive' rather than 'mutually exclusive',[6] 'trade-offs' can be made between them, and the more dominant one of the models is, the less dominant will the others be. The trade-offs that are actually made—and likewise those that could have been made—typically reflect the concerns and bargaining strengths of administrators and officials in the case of the bureaucratic model; professionals and 'street level bureaucrats'[7] in the case of the professional model; lawyers, court and tribunal personnel in the case of the juridical model; managers and auditors in the case of the managerial model; consumers and members of the public in the case of the consumerist model; and private sector providers in the case of the market model. The power struggle between these institutional actors determines the outcome of the trade-offs between the different models of administrative

[6] Halliday (2003) has argued that the managerial, consumerist and market models are not distinct models but are aspects of new public management and are better understood as aspects a single model. However, since each has a distinctive set of characteristics and can exist without the others, I prefer the original formulation.

[7] Lipsky (1980: 3) defines street-level bureaucrats as 'public service workers who interact directly with citizens in the course of their jobs, and who have substantial discretion in the execution of their work'. See, also, Brodkin (2013).

justice with which they are associated and thus the overall administrative justice associated with administrative decision-making in that context.[8]

A study of discretionary decision-making in the implementation of activation policies in Norway provides a good illustration of this approach.[9] As Jesse and Tufte, point out, Michael Lipsky has argued that discretion is an inevitable and continuing component of 'street-level' practices in social welfare administration. On the other hand, critics have pointed out that management reforms have decreased opportunities for exercising discretion through formal regulation and standardisation as managers have seized control over street-level practices. At the same time, new information and communication technology (ICT) is transforming street-level bureaucracies and agencies into 'screen-level bureaucracies' that also decrease opportunities for the exercise of discretion.[10] Based on two surveys of front-line workers and managers, undertaken before and after the integration of local organisations responsible for the implementation of social security and labour-market policy, they provide empirical evidence that throws light on these competing claims. Although the authors do not refer to administrative justice, and their study does not include any external (outsourced) service providers, it is indicative of the role that research can play in throwing light on the impact of organisational change on the justice of administrative decision-making.

The next stage in the argument is to consider the impact of some the changes outlined in previous chapters for the trade-offs between the different normative models outlined above and thus, for the administrative justice encountered in the implementation of benefit sanctions. Five sets of changes, all of which have been described in earlier chapters, which affect the administration of benefit sanctions are considered: the demise of independent adjudication; the creation of Personal Advisers; the introduction of Jobseeker's Agreements and Jobseeker's Directions; the contracting-out of the Work Programme; and the introduction of MR.

---

[8]   Henman and Fenger (2006: 262–263) identify three 'ideal types' of welfare administration: a bureaucratic type, an NPM type and a governance type; which they characterise in terms of their participants, their practices and their processes. However, these models do not focus on the justice of administrative decision-making and are much less fully elaborated than the six models presented in this chapter.

[9]   Jesse and Tufte (2007).

[10]  Landsbergen (2004).

### Change 1: The Demise of Independent Adjudication

Prior to the Social Security Act 1998, the arrangements for decision-making in social insurance were very different from those in social assistance. In social assistance, first-instance decisions were made, in a typically bureaucratic manner, by departmental staff who were accountable to the Secretary of State. They applied the statutory rules to the facts of the case that they were considering. In social insurance, on the other hand, decisions were made by adjudication officers, who were accountable, in a managerial sense, to the Secretary of State, but were expected to act independently in making decisions about whether claimants were entitled to benefit.[11] To the extent that they were accountable for their decisions, their accountability lay, in the first instance, to social security appeal tribunals and, thereafter, to the Social Security Commissioners[12] and the courts. This mode of decision-making embodied a juridical mode of decision-making and the abolition of adjudication officers and their replacement by departmental officials acting on behalf of the Secretary of State in the 1998 Act represented a shift away from the juridical model of administrative justice towards the bureaucratic model, which, at this point, became the dominant model across the social security system. It will be argued that this change has had profound effects on administrative justice in social security, in general, and on the administration of benefit sanctions, in particular.[13]

### Change 2: The Creation of Personal Advisers

When Jobcentre Plus was established, one of its aims was to create a unified workforce from staff who previously worked for the Employment Service or the Benefits Agency.[14] The 'Personal Adviser', who managed a caseload of job-seekers, became the key member of staff.[15] At the service

---

[11] Baldwin et al. (1992).

[12] Predecessors of the Judges who now sit in the Social Entitlement Chamber of the Upper Tribunal.

[13] On the downgrading of independent adjudication and the increasing emphasis on speed and efficiency in the DWP, see Warren (2006).

[14] Analogous developments involving the integration of social security and labour market services and the creation of a single, joined-up service took place in several countries at this time. See Christensen and Lægrid (2007).

[15] See Adler (2008).

level, the merger was associated with the introduction of a more individualised service, in which Personal Advisers would meet claimants to discuss their work aspirations and options; assist them in searching for jobs; explore their training needs and the availability of training programmes; and advise them on childcare and the availability of specialist services. Personal Advisers were not prototypical professionals, like doctors or social workers, who had undertaken a course of professional training. They were, rather, 'street level bureaucrats', like policemen or youth workers, whose expertise was based on their experience in responding to the needs and circumstances of their clients.[16] Personal Advisers embodied a 'professional' mode of decision-making in so far as they had considerable discretion in carrying out their work, and the change represented a shift away from the bureaucratic model of administrative justice, which had been dominant in the Benefits Agency, towards the professional model, which, at this point, became the dominant model across the board.

Attention has been drawn attention to the high degree of discretion that Personal Advisers exercised in advising and supporting sick and disabled Employment and Support Allowance (ESA) claimants,[17] and it can be assumed that they likewise exercised a good deal of discretion in advising unemployed Job Seeker's Allowance (JSA) claimants. It should be noted that discretion based on professional judgement is a hallmark of the professional mode of decision-making but that it is very difficult to challenge.[18]

### Change 3: The Introduction of Jobseeker's Agreements and Jobseeker's Directions

When Jobseeker's Allowance emphasised the responsibility of the unemployed to take advantage of every opportunity offered to them to return to work. Everyone in receipt of JSA was required to enter a 'Jobseekers Agreement', which specified the detailed weekly steps they were expected to take in looking for work. They were also assigned a Personal Adviser (see above) whose role was to provide individualised and continuous support for job-seekers. Personal Advisers were

---

[16] See Lipsky (1980) and Brodkin (2013).
[17] Sainsbury (2008).
[18] Adler (2013).

also responsible for monitoring the claimant's compliance with the requirements set out in the Jobseeker's Agreement at fortnightly intervals, and referring cases to Department for Work and Pensions (DWP) decision-makers in local offices if they thought that the claimant had not applied for or had refused to accept a job vacancy. It was then up to the DWP decision-maker to decide whether to impose a sanction. DWP decision-makers were also given the power to issue a 'Jobseekers Direction', which required those in receipt of JSA to look for jobs in specified ways, take specific steps to 'improve their employability', or take part in a training scheme, and they were empowered to impose sanctions on those who did not meet these requirements.

There must be doubts about the extent to which claimants understand the detail of the Jobseeker's Agreement they have to sign, which can be used to justify the imposition of a sanction if they fail to adhere to its terms. Nevertheless, setting out their responsibilities in this way must contribute to administrative justice because it constrains the discretion of Personal Advisers and the decision-making powers of DWP decision-makers.

### Change 4: The Contracting-Out of the Work Programme

When the Work Programme was introduced in 2011, all job search activities were outsourced to external contractors on a payment-by-results basis. This gave external contractors a much bigger stake in the administration of social security benefits. In spite of it being the flagship welfare-to-work scheme of the 2010–2015 UK Coalition Government, and later of the 2015–2017 Conservative Government, the DWP announced in November 2015 that, because of the fall in unemployment, a programme on this scale was no longer needed, and that it intended to replace the Work Programme with a new Work and Health Programme for the longer-term unemployed and those with chronic health conditions.[19] There have been no new referrals to the Work Programme since February 2017 and the programme officially ended on 1 April 2017. The intention appears to be to run the replacement programme in a similar manner, but it is really too early to say how it will operate.

---

[19] It included claimants in receipt of ESA as well as claimants in receipt of JSA and, subsequently, claimants in receipt of UC.

In addition to helping claimants to find and stay in sustainable work by providing services for them, Work Programme contractors were required to raise 'compliance doubts' with Jobcentre Plus staff when claimants failed to meet one of the conditions set out in their Jobseeker's Agreement, and they would then determine whether the claimant should be sanctioned. The more energetically they did this, the more sanctions would be imposed by DWP decision-makers. Since Work Programme/Work and Health Programme contractors are remunerated on a 'payment by results' basis, it is clearly in their interest if their staff refer 'difficult' or 'uncooperative' claimants to the Job Centre. In fact, this requirement has given rise to concerns, denied by the DWP, that contractors put pressure on staff to increase the number of sanctions in order to concentrate on easy-to-place customers and meet their performance targets.[20]

This process has been analysed in terms of 'creaming' and 'parking'. 'Creaming' refers to provider behaviour that prioritises unemployed claimants with fewer barriers to work who are felt to be easier, cheaper and more likely to move into paid work and release outcome payments. 'Parking' refers to provider behaviour that deliberately neglects allocating time, energy or resources to unemployed claimants with more substantial barriers to work, who are considered to be relatively unlikely to move into paid work and/or to require considerable, and usually expensive, employment support to make a move (and hence an outcome payment) likely. In the Work Programme, providers' incentives to 'cream' and 'park' differently positioned claimants were meant to be 'designed out' by the creation of nine payment groups (based on claimants' prior benefit receipt) into which different claimants were allocated and across which job outcome payments for providers differed. However, evaluation evidence suggests that 'creaming' and 'parking' practices remained common.[21]

The introduction of private contractors into a hitherto wholly public service mode of service delivery reflected a shift away from the largely bureaucratic model of administrative justice towards the managerial and market models with their emphasis on meeting performance targets and payment by results, which, in turn, reflects the emergence of managers

---

[20] See Hegarty (2015).
[21] For more details, see Carter and Whitworth (2015). For an example, see Wright (2006).

and private contractors as institutional players in the administrative justice system. It will be argued that this change has also had a profound effect on the administrative justice of procedures for imposing benefit sanctions.[22]

### Change 5: The Introduction of Mandatory Reconsideration

The procedures for challenging decisions were changed in October 2013 when MR was introduced. Until then, claimants could either ask for the decision to impose a sanction, or any other decision, to be reviewed, in which case, this would be undertaken by a different decision maker, or they could appeal directly to a tribunal. Since October 2013, they have had to first make an informal request for reconsideration. The claimant is then telephoned by the original decision-maker and given a verbal 'explanation' or, on request, a written statement of reasons (WSOR) and may be given an opportunity to provide further information relevant to the decision. If the claimant accepts this explanation, the matter ends there. If, however, the claimant disputes anything, the initial decision-maker will consider what they have to say, including any new evidence they present. The initial decision-maker may change his/her decision at this point but, if not, and the claimant insists, the initial decision maker (not the claimant) should request a formal MR, which is undertaken by a remotely-located Dispute Resolution Team (DRT), and only if this is turned down can the claimant appeal to a tribunal.[23] Claimants who wish to appeal must submit an application to HM Courts and Tribunals Service (HMCTS) within one month of the date on which they were given the result of MR.[24]

There has been no research on why claimants who have challenged the imposition of a sanction through the procedures described above and have had the decision confirmed do not go on to appeal but

---

[22] It also created the potential for fraud and the provision of poor service, and enabled ministers to evade democratic accountability for the programme while the private contractors maximised their profits without incurring any financial risk. See Hodge (2016: Chapter 13).

[23] See Webster (2015).

[24] Under the previous system, claimants submitted their appeals to the DWP which then transferred them to HMCTS. The DWP claimed that this caused delay in arranging tribunals and confusion for claimants who did not know which organisation was responsible for the appeal at any point.

'appeal fatigue'[25] and the length of time it takes for cases to be reconsidered are undoubtedly important explanatory factors. It has meant that the independent element in the overall system of accountability that used to be provided by tribunals has effectively been destroyed.

In some cases, the new system may result in a favourable outcome more quickly, especially if the claimant provides new supporting evidence that supports his/her case. However, while the claimant's case is being reconsidered—and this may take some time because informal and mandatory reconsideration (MR) are not subject to any time limits—those who have been sanctioned do not receive any benefit. The new arrangements have led to an unprecedented fall in the number of appeals against sanctions. After the introduction of MR, appeals to tribunals against sanction decisions for JSA claimants fell from about 3,800 per month to under 100 per month. Across the board, there was a similar reduction in the number of social security appeals. Appeals fell from 40,000 per month to 8,000 per month over a 15-month period.[26] Across the board, there was a similar reduction in the number of social security appeals, which can be seen from Fig. 7.1. Part of the reason for the decline in the number of appeals to the first-tier tribunal was the decline in the number of benefit sanctions imposed by the DWP but the introduction of MR must also have played a role.[27]

One of the consequences of introducing MR and requiring anyone who wished to challenge a decision to impose a sanction was that the proportion of challenges that were upheld fell dramatically. MR success rates are very much lower than appeal tribunal success rates and, almost certainly, lower than they should be. Of the 960,000 MR decided between 2013 and 2016, 166,300 (17%) were allowed.[28] By contrast, success rates for those cases that were taken to a tribunal were much higher at 40–60%.

These outcomes are not those that might have been expected. If MR was an effective means of correcting erroneous decisions, it would be reasonable to assume that erroneous decisions would be screened

---

[25] Cowan and Halliday (2013: 138–140) account for 'claimant fatigue' in terms of the difficult circumstances of claimants' lives which sap their energy to pursue a challenge to the welfare bureaucracy.

[26] See Thomas (2016).

[27] See Chapter 4 above, especially Tables 4.2 and 4.3.

[28] The success rate for MR was initially, in late 2013–early 2014, about 35%, but, when the procedure had 'bedded in', from May 2015 onwards, it stabilised at about 15%.

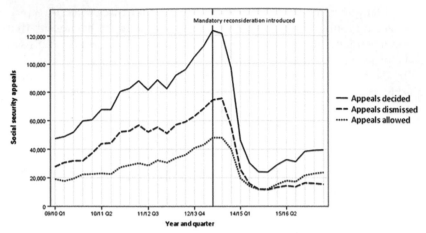

Note: the vertical solid line marks the introduction of mandatory reconsideration in 2013.

**Fig. 7.1** Social security appeals to the first-tier tribunal, 2009–2016 (*Source* Thomas 2016: Fig. 1)

out and few of the cases that are upheld by MR would have the potential to lead to a successful appeal. Since all the cases that are appealed to a tribunal have already been through MR, we would expect few of them to be successful. However, this is the opposite of what occurs in practice.[29]

These are not the outcomes that might have been expected. If MR was an effective means of correcting erroneous decisions, it would be reasonable to assume that few of the cases that emerge from it would have the potential to result in successful appeals. Since all the cases that are appealed to a tribunal have already been through MR, we would expect few of them to lead to a successful appeal. Instead, this is the opposite of what occurs in practice.

The main reason for the difference in appeal rates is that the procedures for MR are different from appeal procedures in two important ways. First, the decision makers are departmental civil servants rather than

[29] The success rate for appeals was initially, in late 2013, about 40% but increased to more than 60% three years later. This was presumably because, over time, the success rates for MR fell and challenges to decisions in meritorious cases were rejected when they should have been upheld.

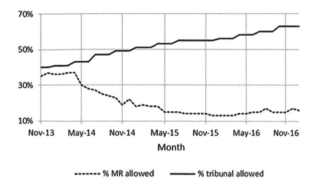

**Fig. 7.2** Outcomes from Mandatory Reconsideration and appeals in social security cases, 2013–2016 (*Source* Thomas 2016: Fig. 2)

independent adjudicators; and, secondly, they approach the task by reviewing decisions, perhaps in the light of further evidence, which have already been taken rather than by taking a new decision based on the evidence put forward by the two parties (the claimant and the DWP) who are in dispute. MR contains an inbuilt bias in favour of the DWP while appeal procedures do not.

The much higher success rate for tribunal appeals compared to MR is clear from Fig. 7.2.

This difference in approach is illustrated by the accounts from claimants of the circumstances that had resulted in a sanction. Under MR, the aim of the review procedure is to determine whether the rules, as set out in the Decision Makers' Guide, have been applied correctly; whereas, in an appeal to an independent tribunal, the aim is to weigh up these competing accounts and/or assess the voracity of the claimant and the validity of the accounts they put forward. These are completely different procedures and it is not surprising that they produce very different outcomes. Moreover, in light of the government's commitment to conditionality and the use of benefit sanctions, it is not really surprising that one of these procedures should have replaced the other.

From the government's perspective, MR has been a great success.[30] As shown in Table 7.2, it has cut the cost of challenging decisions,

---

[30] For a critical assessment of MR, which focuses on its use by the DWP in reviewing social security decisions and by the Home Office in reviewing immigration decisions, and on its implications for administrative justice, see Thomas and Tomlinson (2017).

**Table 7.2** Comparison of Mandatory Reconsideration and tribunal appeals in social security

|  | Mandatory Reconsideration | Tribunal appeals |
|---|---|---|
| Volume (2015/2016) | 317,000 | 131,000 |
| Unit cost | £80.00 | £592.00 |
| Average clearance time (days) | 13 | 119 |
| Success rate (%) | 15 | 55 |

*Source* Data taken from Thomas (2016: Table 2)

speeded up the process and reduced the number of decisions that are reversed. However, from the claimant's perspective, it has reduced the likelihood that a challenge will be successful and increased the length of the overall process. It is therefore not surprising that, of all the transactions claimants have with the Department, MR has the lowest satisfaction rating.[31]

In terms of administrative justice, MR has, once again, increased the influence of the bureaucratic model of administrative justice at the expense of the juridical one.

## IMPLICATIONS FOR ADMINISTRATIVE JUSTICE

The changes set out above can be summarised as follows:

- The demise of independent adjudication promoted the bureaucratic model at the expense of the juridical model of administrative justice.
- The creation of Personal Advisers promoted a professional model at the expense of the bureaucratic model[32] by professionalising jobsearch and training in line with the government's commitment to conditionality.

---

[31] Department for Work and Pensions, *DWP Claimant Service and Experience Survey 2014/15* (2016: 85).

[32] Wright (2006: 164) identifies the emergence of a new class of 'bureau-professionals'.

- The introduction of Jobseeker's Agreements promoted the bureaucratic model at the expense of the professional one by limiting the decision maker's discretion and promoting more consistent decisions.
- The contracting-out of the Work Programme promoted the managerial and market models at the expense of the professional model and provided incentives for providers to refer 'hard-to-place' claimants to decision-makers to consider whether a sanction should be imposed.
- The introduction of MR promoted the bureaucratic model at the expense of the juridical model by making it more difficult to challenge the imposition of a sanction and less likely that such a challenge would succeed.

These changes have affected the six models of administrative justice in different ways

The importance of the **bureaucratic model** increased in some ways but decreased in others. It gained in importance following the demise of independent adjudication and the introduction of MR but lost out through the introduction of Personal Advisers and the professionalisation of job-search and training activities, and from the contracting out of the Work Programme. Its main champions are DWP decision makers in local Jobcentre Plus offices.

The importance of the **professional model** also experienced a series of swings and roundabouts. It increased in importance following the introduction of Personal Advisers and the professionalisation of job-search and training activities but decreased as a result of the introduction of Jobseeker's Agreements. Its main champions are front-line staff employed by Work Programme providers.

The importance of the **juridical model** declined as that of other models increased. Its importance decreased, first, as a result of the demise of independent adjudication and, subsequently from the introduction of MR since this led to a much-reduced role for appeal tribunals. Its main champions are advice agencies and tribunal judges.

The **managerial and market models** can be considered together since they both received a considerable boost from the out-sourcing of the Work Programme and the contracting-out of training and job search. Private contractors became a new set of institutional actors in the administrative justice system and had a considerable influence on it. Its main champions are managers employed by Work Programme providers.

There was little or no evidence of the **consumerist model** and it is fair to assume that it has had little impact on the administration of social security benefits in recent years.

## IMPLICATIONS FOR BENEFIT SANCTIONS

Although the arguments in this chapter apply 'across the board' in social security, it is reasonable to assume that they apply to the imposition of benefit sanctions and to the procedures for challenging them.

The DWP has produced a schematic account of the different stages in the decision-making process leading up to the possible imposition of a benefit sanction (see Fig. 7.3). However, it does not describe how the process works in practice or how sanctioning decisions are actually made. It would be very instructive to conduct some empirical research that would throw light on the roles of the various actors in the system and the ways in which, as they seek to promote the particular model of administrative justice with which they are associated, i.e. research on how

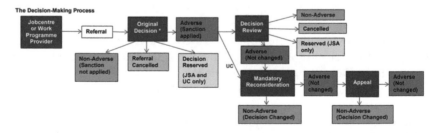

**Fig. 7.3**    The decision-making process for benefit sanctions (*Source* Department for Work and Pensions (2017). *Benefit Sanctions Statistics,* June 3, available at https://www.gov.uk/government/uploads/system/uploads/attachment_data/file/661218/benefit-sanctions-statistics-to-june-2017.pdf)

they shape the process of making, reviewing and reconsidering decisions to sanction claimants.[33]

## CONCLUSION: JUSTICE AND FAIRNESS IN ADMINISTRATION

The type of justice found in the administration of benefit sanctions is the outcome of a struggle for ascendancy and control between DWP decision makers in local offices, front-line staff and managers employed by outsourced Work Programme providers, advice agencies and tribunal judges, and the trade-offs between the different models of administrative justice with which each of them is associated. The changing fortunes of administrative justice in the UK can be likened to the swing of a pendulum.[34] The passage of the Tribunals, Courts and Enforcement Act (TCEA) and the establishment of the Administrative Justice and Tribunals Council (AJTC) in 2007 represented its high point but the abolition of the AJTC in 2013, cuts in funding to legal aid and for the provision of legal advice, and the channelling of disputes into internal review procedures rather than external rights of appeal reflect its rapid decline, all of which have implications for challenging the imposition of benefit sanctions.[35]

## REFERENCES

Adler, M. (2006). Fairness in Context. *Journal of Law and Society, 33*(4), 615–638.

Adler, M. (2008). The Justice Implications of Activation Policies in the UK. In S. Stendahl, T. Erhag, & S. Devetzi (Eds.), *A European Work-First Welfare State*. Gothenburg: Centre for European Research, University of Gothenburg.

---

[33] The collection of papers published in Brodkin and Marston (2013) illustrate the potential of empirical research on decision-making in welfare to work programmes.

[34] Adler (2012).

[35] The recent announcement that the all-party law-reform and human rights organisation *Justice* is to host a new Administrative Justice Council as a successor to the AJTC does offer a glimmer of hope. The new body will have oversight of the whole of the administrative justice system in the UK, advising governments, including the devolved governments, and the judiciary about its development. However, it will have fewer resources than the AJTC and will not have any comparable statutory powers. See press release at https://justice.org.uk/justice-host-successor-administrative-justice-forum/.

Adler, M. (2010). Understanding and Analysing Administrative Justice. In M. Adler (Ed.), *Administrative Justice in Context*. Oxford: Hart Publishing.

Adler, M. (2012). The Rise and Fall of Administrative Justice—A Cautionary Tale. *Socio-Legal Review, 8*(2), 28–54.

Adler, M. (2013). Conditionality, Sanctions and the Effective Absence of Redress in the British "New Deal" Programs. In E. Z. Brodkin & G. Marston (Eds.), *Work and the Welfare State: The Politics and Management of Policy Change* (pp. 229–248). Washington, DC: Georgetown University Press; Copenhagen: DJØF.

Baldwin, J., Wikeley, N., & Young, R. (1992). *Judging Social Security Claims*. Oxford: Clarendon Press.

Brodkin, E. Z. (2013). Work and the Welfare State. In E. Z. Brodkin & G. Marston (Eds.), *Work and the Welfare State: The Politics and Management of Policy Change*. Washington, DC: Georgetown University Press; Copenhagen: DJØF.

Brodkin, E. Z., & Marston, G. (Eds.). (2013). *Work and the Welfare State: The Politics and Management of Policy Change*. Washington, DC: Georgetown University Press; Copenhagen: DJØF.

Carter, E., & Whitworth, A. (2015). Creaming and Parking in Quasi-Marketised Welfare-to-Work Schemes: Designed-Out of or Designed-Into the UK Work Programme? *Journal of Social Policy, 44*(2), 277–296.

Christensen, T., & Lægrid, P. (2007). The Whole-of-Government Approach to Public Sector Reform. *Public Administration Review, 67*(6), 1059–1066.

Cowan, D., & Halliday, S. (2003). *The Appeal of Internal Review: Law, Administrative Justice, and the (Non-)Emergence of Disputes*. Oxford and Portland, OR: Hart Publishing.

Department for Work and Pensions. (2016). *DWP Claimant Service and Experience Survey 2014/15*. London. Available at https://www.gov.uk/government/uploads/system/uploads/attachment_data/file/498207/rr916-dwp-claimant-service-and-experience-survey.pdf.

Genn, H. (2010). *Judging Civil Justice*. Cambridge: Cambridge University Press.

Halliday, S. (2003). *Judicial Review and Compliance with Administrative Law*. Oxford: Hart Publishing.

Hegarty, P. (2015, February 4). Work Programme Staff Were Told to Sanctions Against Clients. *New Statesman*.

Henman, P., & Fenger, M. (2006). Reforming Welfare Governance: Reflections. In P. Henman & M. Fenger (Eds.), *Administering Welfare Reform: International Transformations in Welfare Governance* (pp. 257–278). Bristol: Policy Press.

Hodge, M. (2016). *Called to Account*. London: Abacus.

Jesse, J. T., & Tufte, P. A. (2007). Discretionary Decision-Making in a Changing Context of Activation Policies and Welfare Reforms. *Journal of Social Policy, 43*(2), 269–288.

Landsbergen, D. (2004). Screen Level Bureaucracy: Databases as Public Records. *Government Information Quarterly, 21,* 25–50.

Lipsky, M. (1980). *Street-Level Bureaucracy: Dilemmas of the Individual in Public Services.* New York: Russell Sage Foundation.

Mashaw, J. L. (1983). *Bureaucratic Justice: Managing Social Security.* New Haven and London: Yale University Press.

Richardson, G. (1984). The Legal Regulation of Process. In G. Richardson & H. Genn (Eds.), *Administrative Law and Government Action* (pp. 105–130). Oxford: Clarendon Press.

Sainsbury, R. (2008). Administrative Justice, Discretion and the 'Welfare to Work' Project. *Journal of Social Welfare and Family Law, 30*(4), 323–338.

Thomas, R. (2016). *The New Administrative Review: Administrative Justice in a Cold Climate.* Unpublished Paper.

Thomas, R., & Tomlinson, J. (2017). Mapping Current Issues in Administrative Justice: Austerity and the 'More Bureaucratic Rationality' Approach. *Journal of Social Welfare and Family Law, 39*(3), 380–399.

Warren, N. (2006). The Adjudication Gap: A Discussion Document. *Journal of Social Security Law, 13*(2), 110–118.

Webster, D. (2015, May 13). *Briefing: The DWP's JSA/ESA Sanctions Statistics Release.* Available at http://www.cpag.org/david-webster.

Wright, S. (2006). The Administration of Transformation: A Case Study of Implementing Welfare Reform in the UK. In P. Henman & M. Fenger (Eds.), *Administering Welfare Reform: International Transformations in Welfare Governance* (pp. 161–182). Bristol: Policy Press.

CHAPTER 8

# The Role of Law in Protecting the Right to a Social Minimum

Given the weakness of the juridical model of administrative justice, and the very small number of cases involving benefit sanctions that have been taken to a tribunal, it is not surprising that the law has provided very few checks on the imposition of benefit sanctions and very little protection for those who are subject to them. If few cases are appealed to a first-instance tribunal, there will be a very small pool of cases that could be taken forward to the Upper Tribunal and the courts. Thus, there is little scope for the courts to test the legality of practices that leave many people destitute. In this chapter, we consider the role played by the courts in the small number of cases dealing with job search requirements and benefit sanctions that they have considered and assess the extent to which international conventions have been effective in protecting the rights of claimants to a basic minimum.

## THE EUROPEAN CONVENTION ON HUMAN RIGHTS (ECHR)

In 2005, in a case brought by two asylum seekers,[1] who were refused support under the Nationality, Immigration and Asylum Act on the grounds that they had made a late claim, the House of Lords held that the failure to provide them with support exposed them to a real risk of destitution and that this constituted a violation of Article 3 of the

---

[1] R *(Adam and Limbuela) v Secretary of State for the Home Department* [2015] UKHL 66.

© The Author(s) 2018
M. Adler, *Cruel, Inhuman or Degrading Treatment?*, Palgrave
Socio-Legal Studies, https://doi.org/10.1007/978-3-319-90356-9_8

European Convention of Human Rights (ECHR). In light of this, one might have expected that the courts would likewise have found benefit sanction to constitute a violation of Article 3 but this has not been tested in the courts. Two cases that have reached the superior courts have questioned the legality of conditionality in terms of its compatibility with the ECHR but neither of them have been based on Article 3.

The first case (*Reilly No. 1*)[2] concerned the Jobseeker's Allowance (JSA) (Employment, Skills and Enterprise Scheme) Regulations 2011 (SI 2011/917) and, in particular, that of the 'work experience' and 'training' programmes, which claimants had to take part in as a condition of receiving benefit and for which they would be sanctioned if they failed to do so. The case focused on the legality of the regulations that established the training programme and on their compatibility with Article 4.

In the High Court, the judge found that the regulations were validly made but the decision was over-ruled in the Court of Appeal, which found that they were *ultra vires* because the claimants were not provided with an adequate description of the programmes or the circumstances in which they could be required to participate in them as required by the primary legislation. However, the Court of Appeal rejected the Article 4 part of the claim, arguing that 'to amount to a violation of Article 4, the work had to be not only compulsory and involuntary, but the obligation to work, or its performance, must be "unjust", "oppressive", "an avoidable hardship" [or] "needlessly distressing"'. The Court of Appeal did not consider that the imposition of the work condition in this case, which was intended to support the purpose for which the conditional benefit was provided, met the starting point for a possible contravention of Article 4. The Court of Appeal's decision was subsequently upheld by the UK Supreme Court, which held that the conditions imposed on recipients of JSA 'come nowhere close to exploitative conduct at which Article 4 is aimed'.

The second case (*Reilly No. 2*)[3] concerned the legality of being required to participate in the unpaid work scheme that had been declared *ultra vires* in the first case, in spite of the fact that the Secretary of State for Work and Pensions had introduced new regulations with retrospective effect. The two claimants submitted that the new legislation was

[2]   R *(Reilly and Wilson) v Secretary of State for Work and Pensions* [2013] 1 WLR 1 2239; [2013] EWCA Civ; [2013] UKSC 68, paras 83 and 90 (*'Reilly No. 1'*). See Larkin (2013).

[3]   R *(on the application of Reilly and Hewstone) v Secretary of State for Work and Pensions* [2016] EWHC Civ 413 (*'Reilly No 2'*). For a commentary on this case, see Larkin (2015).

incompatible with their rights to a fair hearing under Article 6 of the ECHR and one of them, who had been sanctioned, also argued that, by withholding his benefit, the Secretary of State had deprived him of a 'possession' to which he had a right under Article 1 of Protocol 1 (A1P1) of the EHCR and that this could not be justified 'in the public interest'.

The Court of Appeal held that '... an interference with Article 6 rights can only be justified "by compelling grounds of public interest"'. In their decision, the Court of Appeal concluded that there were no 'compelling grounds of general interest' to justify the interference with the Article 6 rights and that there had been a violation of Article 6. However, they asserted that this only applied to the minority of claimants who had pursued claims in the courts or tribunals. On the A1P1 point, the Court of Appeal held that the claimant was not deprived of a possession merely because he was not able to receive the benefit in the future due to the application of the sanction. The claimant did not have a property right to future benefits because he did not meet the required conditions to be able to continue to receive the benefit: 'in order to establish a property right, the applicant must fulfil the requirements for receipt of the benefit at the relevant time' and 'the sanction decisions were effective and lawful unless or until overturned'.

To sum up, although *Reilly No. 1* and *Reilly No. 2* were successful on procedural grounds, in that the two appeals were partially upheld, the attempts to invoke the ECHR to declare aspects of conditionality and the imposition of sanctions unlawful were unsuccessful. Two further cases reached the superior courts but neither made any reference to the ECHR and both were unsuccessful.

## The International Covenant on Economic, Social and Cultural Rights (ICESCR) and the European Social Charter (ESC)

The ICESCR and the ESC impose restrictions on the reduction, suspension or termination of social assistance due to work-related sanctions.[4] Article 9 of the ICESCR recognises the right of everyone to social security, while Article 11 recognises, among other things, the right of

---

[4] This account of the ICESCR and the ESC makes extensive use of a more detailed account by Eleveld (2016).

everyone to an adequate standard of living. In 2015, the UN Committee on Economic, Social and Cultural Rights (CESCR), the supervisory body for the ICESCR, declared that basic social security guarantees 'constitute the core obligation of ratifying states to ensure access to social security by providing, together with adequate access to essential services, a minimum level of benefits to all individuals and families to enable them to acquire at least essential health care, basic shelter and housing, water and sanitation, food and the most basic forms of education'.

The CESCR seeks to ensure universal access to a minimum level of benefits. In addition, it has argued that, at the expiry of the period of entitlement to unemployment benefit, the social security system should ensure adequate protection, for example through a system of social assistance. In this regard it has expressed its concerns regarding the imposition of work-related conditions in social assistance for disadvantaged claimants. For example, in a recent report, it urged the UK Government to reconsider 'the eligibility criteria for social assistance benefits insofar as they affect the most disadvantaged and marginalised groups.[5]

Compared to the CESCR, the European Committee on Social Rights (ECSR), which is the supervisory body for the European Social Charter (ESC), has been more explicit when it comes to work-related conditionality and sanctioning in social assistance. The right to social assistance enshrined in Article 13(1) of the ESC states that, 'with a view to ensuring the effective exercise of the right to social [and medical] assistance, state parties undertake to ensure that any person who is without adequate resources and who is unable to secure such resources either by his own efforts or from other sources, be granted adequate assistance'. This is closely related to comparable provisions in other international treaties and, on several occasions, the ECSR has stated that the ESC should be interpreted in harmony with other rules of international law implying, among other things, that the ECSR interprets Article 13(1) in conformity with the minimum core obligations of the ICESR, such as the right to be free from hunger. In addition, it has imposed three restrictions on the reduction, suspension or termination of entitlement to social assistance due to a (work-related) benefit sanction: first, the conditions should be 'reasonable and consistent with the aim pursued, that is to say to finding a lasting solution to the individual's difficulties';

---

[5]   CESCR, Concluding observations on the sixth periodic report of the United Kingdom of Great Britain and Northern Ireland, E/C.12/GBR/CO/6, 14 July 2016, para 40.

second, reduction, suspension or termination should 'not deprive the person concerned of his/her means of subsistence'; and, third, 'it must be possible to appeal against a decision to suspend or reduce assistance'.

With respect to the first restriction ('reasonable and consistent with the aim pursued'), the ECSR does not usually assess whether the work requirements in social assistance regulations are 'reasonable and consistent with the aim of finding a lasting solution to the individual's difficulties'. However, the evidence reviewed in Chapter 6, which demonstrated how one effect of benefit sanctions in the UK is to force claimants into a 'no person's land' in which they are neither in work nor on benefit, and which made it clear that benefit sanctions impose a great deal of hardship on those who are subject to them, suggests that the main reason for introducing them has been to make dependence on benefits as unattractive as possible. Whether benefit sanctions in the UK meet the requirements of the ESC would appear to be rather doubtful.

With respect to the second point ('not to deprive the person concerned of his/her means of subsistence'), the ECSR has frequently asked ratifying states to provide additional information to assess whether a sanctioned recipient still has access to adequate means of subsistence. In the case of the UK, in its 2013 Report, the ECSR asked further questions concerning the hardship clauses in Jobseeker's Allowance legislation. It noted that, under the Welfare Reform Act 2012, benefit sanctions were strengthened, and hardship payments were restricted to those claimants in greatest need, and asked the UK Government to clarify the criteria that would be applied in practice to ensure that, in conformity with the ESC, a person would not be deprived of his/her means of subsistence.[6] The UK Government has not yet responded and whether the system of hardship payments (discussed in Chapter 6) meets the ECSR's expectations has not been determined. Likewise, whether the demise of independent adjudication following the introduction of MR (also discussed in Chapter 6) has undermined the ECSR's requirement that it must be possible to appeal against the imposition of a benefit sanction is still an open question. The UN Committee on CESCR also raised serious concerns about the reliance on sanctions in the UK without appropriate access to justice or due process for those affected.[7]

---

[6] European Social Charter, European Committee of Social Rights 2013 (2014) Conclusions XX-2, United Kingdom—Article 13(1), 29 January. For a commentary, see Cashman (2014).

[7] Noyce (2016). For a general discussion, see Simpson (2018).

The main problems with the rights enshrined in the ICESR and the ESC is that, in the UK, they are non-justiciable and non-enforceable. This is not because they are intrinsically non-justiciable or non-enforceable—if the UK Parliament were to enact legislation making them justiciable and enforceable they would be. Their justiciability is limited because domestic mechanisms for implementing economic, social and cultural (ESC) rights, as prescribed in international conventions and charters, are inadequate.[8]

There is some concern that *ex-post* mechanisms, in which aggrieved individuals appeal to the courts, undermine parliamentary sovereignty and that government and parliament are better placed to deal with complex matters like economic and social rights that involve competing priorities and the allocation of scarce resources. However, combining *ex-post* mechanisms with *ex-ante* mechanisms that ensure that government and parliament assess the compatibility of policy and legislation with the international standards that the UK has signed up to, could ensure that appeals to the courts are only used as a last resort. Three *ex-ante* mechanisms have been proposed: giving constitutional status to ESC rights in the same way as it has been given to ECHR rights; imposing a duty on government and parliament to comply with international standards (and allowing the courts to make declarations of incompatibility where this is not the case); and imposing a duty on them to 'have due regard' to the rights contained in these international treaties.[9]

In theory, governments are answerable to the bodies that supervise the international conventions to which they have signed up. In practice, the demands that are currently made of governments are very weak, the possibilities for delay are endless, with the result that governments seem to have had a free hand. As matters stand, violations of economic and social rights—including the right to social security—are widespread and are neither subject to *ex-ante* constraints nor to *ex-post* challenges in the UK.

## Conclusion: The Feebleness of Legal Protection

As demonstrated in this chapter, violations of economic and social rights—including the right to social security—are widespread and are not currently subject to any effective remedies in the UK. The international; conventions that the UK Government has signed up to have not provided any significant protection to claimants who are subjected to oppressive conditions or sanctions that have left them destitute. Where then on the scale of injustice do benefit sanctions in the UK lie? Based on the evidence presented in the previous chapter, which drew attention to the erosion of the right to appeal to an independent tribunal, and in this chapter, which has drawn attention to the failure of the courts to protect the right to a social minimum and the government's unwillingness to confer the same status on economic and social rights as it has conferred on civil and political rights, it would appear that justice was not the primary consideration for those who were responsible for the design or implementation of benefit sanctions.

## References

Boyle, K., & Hughes, E. (2018). Identifying Routes to Remedy for Violations of Economic, Social and Cultural Rights. *International Journal of Human Rights, 22*(1), 43–69.

Cashman, D. (2014). Not Reaping the Benefits: The United Kingdom's Continuing Violation of Article 12(1) of the European Social Charter. *Oxford Human Rights Law Blog.* Available at http://ohrh.law.ox.ac.uk/not-reaping-the-benefits-the-united-kingdoms-continuing-violation-of-article-12%C2%A71-of-the-european-social-charter/.

Eleveld, A. (2016). *Work-Related Sanctions in European Welfare States: An Incentive to Work or a Violation of Minimum Subsistence Rights?* (SSRN Research Paper 2016/01). Amsterdam: The Amsterdam Centre for Contemporary European Studies. Available at https://papers.ssrn.com/sol3/papers.cfm?abstract_id=2802656.

Larkin, P. (2013). A Permanent Blow to Workfare in the United Kingdom or a Temporary Obstacle? Reilly and Wilson v Secretary of State for Work and Pensions. *Journal of Social Security Law, 20*(3), 110–118.

Larkin, P. (2015). Engaging with the Human Rights Angle: Reilly (No. 2) v Secretary of State for Work and Pensions. *Journal of Social Security Law, 22*(2), 85–94.

Noyce, H. (2016, June 30). *UK Human Rights Blog.* Available at https://ukhumanrightsblog.com/2016/06/30/un-committee-seriously-concerned-about-the-impact-of-austerity-on-human-rights.

Simpson, M. (2018, forthcoming). Assessing the Compliance of the UK Social Security System with the State's Obligations under the European Social Charter. *European Human Rights Law Review.*

Wolffe, W. J. (2014, December). *Economic and Social Rights in Scotland: Lessons from the Past: Options for the Future.* A Lecture for International Human Rights Day 2014. Edinburgh Law School. Available at http://www.scottishhumanrights.com/media/1469/wolffe2014lecture.pdf.

# CHAPTER 9

# A Comparison of Benefit Sanctions with Court Fines

The aim of this chapter is to compare the largely unseen phenomenon of benefit sanctions in the UK with the much better known and more visible phenomenon of court fines and, by so doing, to gain a better understanding of what makes benefit sanctions problematic. The chapter starts with an account of the history of court fines, which is intended to complement the account, in Chapter 3, of the history of benefit sanctions, but, as in Chapter 3, attention is focused on recent developments. Time series data for the two monetary penalties are analysed and, at the end of the chapter, their salient characteristics are compared.

## THE HISTORY OF MONETARY SANCTIONS—THE TWENTIETH CENTURY INHERITANCE

In the UK, the use of the fine as a sentencing option in the criminal courts increased throughout the twentieth century, especially in the period after the Second World War.[1] This was, in part, due to the realisation that short terms of imprisonment were counterproductive and, in part, to the fact that an increasing number of offenders earned enough to enable them to pay a fine, especially if they opted to pay by instalments.[2]

---

[1] Fines had, of course, been used prior to the twentieth century, mainly in conjunction with imprisonment. However, from the late nineteenth century onwards, fines came to be used as a sentence in their own right. See O'Malley (2009).

[2] Walker (1968: 230).

© The Author(s) 2018                                           115
M. Adler, *Cruel, Inhuman or Degrading Treatment?*, Palgrave Socio-Legal Studies, https://doi.org/10.1007/978-3-319-90356-9_9

By the 1960s, over 1 million fines per year were imposed by the criminal courts and the number remained at about this level until the end of the century. As a proportion of sentences, fines rose from about 45% of disposals for adult male offenders in 1960 to around 60% in the mid-1970s.[3]

In 1960, fixed penalties were introduced for a number of minor parking and motoring offences. By paying the penalty prescribed for the offence directly into the court, the offender could thereby avoid prosecution. The use of fixed penalties was subsequently extended to cover a wide range of motoring offences, for example speeding offences, as well as anti-social behaviour offences, public order offences and environmental offences, for example littering, and the number of fixed penalties increased year-on-year. By the end of the century, about 4.5 million fixed penalties per year were imposed for motoring offences alone, i.e. four and a half times the number of fines imposed in the criminal courts.

The Road Traffic Act 1991 led to the decriminalisation of parking-related offences throughout the UK and the replacement of criminal sanctions by administrative sanctions. At the request of a local authority, responsibility for parking wardens could be transferred from the police to the local authority and, as a result, fixed penalties paid to the courts were replaced by administrative penalties, known as penalty charge notices (PCNs), paid to the local authority. By the end of the century, about 4 million PCNs per year were being issued in England and Wales alone.[4] In addition, more than 450,000 PCNs per year were being issued in Scotland.

Recent trends in the number of court fines will now be compared with recent trends in the number of benefit sanctions.

## MONETARY SANCTIONS IN THE TWENTY-FIRST CENTURY

### Court Fines

The fine is clearly the most frequently imposed of the sentencing options used in the criminal courts—over the period 2001–2016, around two thirds of those who were sentenced in England and Wales were fined with the remainder sentenced to immediate custody, given

---

[3]   Ashworth (2010: 327).

[4]   Department of Transport (2012) *Civil Parking Enforcement Statistics*, London: Table CPE0101.

**Table 9.1**  Fines imposed by the criminal courts (England and Wales), 2001–2016

| Year | Total number sentenced | Number of fines imposed | Change since 2001 (%) | Number of fines as proportion of sentences (%) | Number given immediate custody | Custody as proportion of sentences (%) |
|------|------|------|------|------|------|------|
| 2001 | 1,348,494 | 930,121 | | 68.97 | 106,273 | 7.88 |
| 2002 | 1,419,608 | 972,737 | +4.58 | 70.44 | 111,607 | 7.86 |
| 2003 | 1,489,827 | 1,033,617 | +11.13 | 69.38 | 106,670 | 7.16 |
| 2004 | 1,547,352 | 1,082,690 | +11.64 | 69.95 | 106,322 | 6.88 |
| 2005 | 1,482,453 | 1,025,064 | +10.20 | 69.14 | 101,236 | 6.83 |
| 2006 | 1,420,571 | 961,535 | +3.38 | 67.69 | 96,017 | 6.76 |
| 2007 | 1,414,742 | 941,534 | +1.22 | 66.55 | 95,206 | 6.73 |
| 2008 | 1,362,064 | 890,296 | −4.28 | 65.36 | 99,525 | 7.31 |
| 2009 | 1,406,905 | 946,146 | +1.72 | 67.25 | 100,231 | 7.12 |
| 2010 | 1,365,347 | 893,931 | −3.89 | 65.47 | 101,513 | 7.43 |
| 2011 | 1,312,739 | 856,808 | −7.88 | 65.26 | 106,150 | 8.09 |
| 2012 | 1,239,827 | 823,298 | −11.48 | 66.40 | 98,047 | 7.91 |
| 2013 | 1,170,000 | 795,600 | −14.46 | 68.00 | 93,000 | 8.33 |
| 2014 | 1,215,695 | 853,335 | −8.26 | 70.19 | 91,140 | 7.47 |
| 2015 | 1,265,137 | 891,918 | −4.18 | 70.50 | 89,822 | 7.10 |
| 2016 | 1,238,035 | 910,644 | −2.09 | 73.56 | 89,812 | 7.25 |

*Source* Ministry of Justice (various years) *Criminal Justice Statistics (England and Wales)*

a suspended sentence, sentenced to a community disposal, given an absolute or conditional discharge or dealt with in some other way.[5] The annual number of fines imposed was remarkably stable over the period although, if the small reduction in the number of people receiving a sentence of any kind is taken into account, the proportion who received a fine increased slightly. The detailed figures are set out in Table 9.1.

## Benefit Sanctions

As noted in Chapter 4, just over 300,000 benefit sanctions were imposed by DWP decision-makers on JSA claimants in 2001. This figure

[5] Ministry of Justice (2001–2016) *Criminal Justice Statistics Quarterly*, December (several years), London, available at https://www.gov.uk/government/statistics/criminal-justice-system-statistics-quarterly-december.

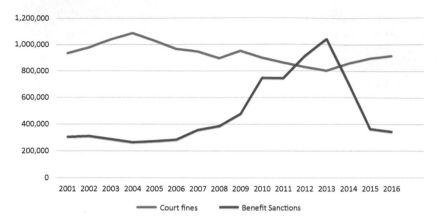

**Fig. 9.1** The incidence of court fines and benefit sanctions, 2001–2016 (*Source* Ministry of Justice (2001–2006) *Criminal Justice Statistics Quarterly* (for court fines); Department for Work and Pensions (2001–2016) *Jobseeker's Allowance and Employment and Support Allowance Sanctions*)

remained stable for the next five years but started to rise quite sharply in 2006 and peaked at over 1,000,000 in 2013 before falling back to 350,000 in 2015 and 340,000 in 2016. Thus, there was a 300+% increase over the period 2001–2013 and a corresponding decrease over the period 2013–2016. In addition to these JSA sanctions, about 34,000 sanctions were imposed on ESA claimants in 2013.[6] The detailed figures were set out in Table 4.2 above.

The total number of benefit sanctions imposed by the DWP over-took the number of fines imposed in the criminal courts in 2013 and, although it fell back in 2014, it was still at a higher level than it was in 2001. This can be seen from Fig. 9.1.

## Assessing the Current State of Play—From a Monopoly to a Mixed Economy

Until 50 years ago, the criminal courts had a monopoly over the imposition of monetary penalties but there is now a mixed economy in which criminal sanctions coexist with monetary penalties that are imposed administratively.

---

[6]   For a more detailed analysis, see Chapter 4 above.

Over time, the number of fines imposed by the criminal courts has been dwarfed by the number of parking penalties imposed by local authorities and, for a few years, it was edged into third place behind the number of benefit sanctions imposed on claimants by the Department for Work and Pensions. This development reflects a 'punitive turn' in social security, analogous to the punitive turn in penal policy and criminal justice.[7]

### The Place of Adjudication

One important difference between fines imposed by the courts and sanctions imposed administratively is that, in the first case, where the offender wishes to challenge the charge by entering a not-guilty plea, adjudication precedes the imposition of the penalty, i.e. the person who is given a fine has either pleaded guilty or been found guilty by the court.[8] This is not the case with administrative sanctions like the benefit sanctions, which DWP decision-makers are empowered to impose. However, those who are subject to benefit sanctions can challenge them by requesting a review from the DWP and, subsequently, by appealing to an independent tribunal. The key difference is that, while adjudication *precedes* the imposition of criminal sanctions, it *follows* the imposition of administrative sanctions. In the case of criminal sanctions, procedural protection is provided by court proceedings; in the case of administrative sanctions, it is, at least notionally, provided by Mandatory Reconsideration (MR) and appeal procedures and, in the analysis below, an attempt is made to assess how adequate these arrangements are.

---

[7]   Garland (2001: 142) used the term 'punitive turn' to refer to '[h]arsher sentencing and increased use of imprisonment, "three strikes" and mandatory minimum sentencing laws; "truth in sentencing" and parole release restrictions; "no frills" prison laws and "austere prisons"; retribution in juvenile courts and the imprisonment of children; the revival of chain gangs and corporal punishment; boot camps and "supermax" prisons; the multiplication of capital offences and executions; community notification laws and paedophile registers; zero tolerance policies and Anti-Social Behaviour Orders (ASBOs)' and claimed that '[t]here is now a long list of measures that appear to signify a punitive turn in contemporary penality.' It is the author's contention that the massive increase in the incidence and severity of benefit sanctions reflected a punitive turn in social security. For other examples of the 'punitive turn' in social security, see Larkin (2007).

[8]   It is, of course, possible for those who are fined to appeal—both against conviction and against sentence—but this option is only taken up in a minority of cases.

In light of these differences, the types of justice that are exemplified by the two types of sanction compared in this chapter can now be considered.[9]

## PROPORTIONALITY

Proportionality requires that the penalty should 'fit the crime', not in the sense of 'an eye for an eye, and a tooth for a tooth' but in the sense that the relationship between the penalty and the crime should be commensurate.[10] This means not only that less serious offences should receive less severe penalties while more serious offences should receive more severe ones, but also that the penalty should be neither more nor less severe than is appropriate. However, it also requires that the penalty should take into account the offender's circumstances. Thus penalties should neither be unduly lenient for people in advantageous circumstances nor unduly harsh for those in less fortunate circumstances. The issue of proportionality is considered first for court fines and then for benefit sanctions.

### *Court Fines*

Fines are imposed by the criminal courts on accused persons who are guilty of a crime or an offence, either as a result of pleading guilty or because they have been found guilty in a trial. For summary offences, there is a standard scale of fines. When a fine is imposed, the court will make a 'collection order' that contains details of how it should be paid. This may allow the fine to be paid in instalments, and where the offender agrees, by means of an attachment of earnings order or a deduction from benefits order that enable instalments to be automatically deducted from wages or benefits and paid into the court.

A standard scale is intended to ensure that the fine imposed is related to the severity of the offence. But, because sentencers do not routinely inquire into offenders' circumstances or ability to pay, and because many offenders are unemployed and/or poor, the extent of proportionality in imposing fines is not very high. Although this is mitigated, to some

---

[9] For a discussion of proportionality in the sentencing of criminal offenders, see von Hirsch and Ashworth (2005), especially Chapter 9 entitled 'Criteria for Proportionality: A Review'.

[10] For a more general discussion, see Adler (2008).

extent, by the arrangements for paying fines by instalments, described above, fine default is quite a serious problem and, although it is being tackled, a few fine defaulters do still end up in prison. It is reasonable to conclude that court fines have a 'moderate' impact on offenders.

Following the *Cawley* judgment,[11] which made it clear that, before imprisoning a fine defaulter, courts in England and Wales must be satisfied that the default is due to the offender's wilful refusal or culpable neglect to pay. In England and Wales, the number of fine defaulters imprisoned for defaulting on fines declined by 70% following the *Cawley* judgment and, since 2001, it has remained fairly steady at about 100 per year.[12] In Scotland, although the number of fine defaulters who are sent to prison has declined from about 8,000 per year at the beginning of the decade, it is still over 1,000 per year. Taking population into account, this means that the Scottish rate is about 500 times higher than the English rate.[13]

In the UK today, offenders who have committed more serious crimes are, by and large, sentenced to imprisonment or given a community disposal while offenders who have committed less serious crimes are sentenced to a fine. As far as the fine itself is concerned, more serious crimes are, on the whole, given larger fines while less serious crimes are given smaller ones. So far, so good. Although, in sentencing an offender, the judge (or the magistrate) will be aware of the offender's criminal record, he/she does not necessarily know anything about the offenders' circumstances or ability to pay.[14] This situation frequently leads to fine default which, as noted above, can still result in imprisonment.

The problems enumerated above are all soluble, for example through the provision of more and better information for sentencers on the financial circumstances of offenders. The conclusion reached here is that, although there are still problems, fines are not, in principle, inconsistent with justice.

### Benefit Sanctions

Benefit sanctions are imposed by DWP decision-makers on claimants who are referred to them by front-line DWP staff in Job Centres and by

---

[11]  R. v. *Oldham Justices ex parte Cawley* [1996] 1 All ER 464.

[12]  Ministry of Justice (2013).

[13]  Scottish Government (2012), Table A9 at 18.

[14]  See Comptroller and Auditor General Office (2006) and Comptroller and Auditor General Office (2007).

those organisations that were contracted under the Work Programme to get the long-term unemployed into work. This gave the DWP an incentive to impose sanctions because they could be incorporated into performance targets.[15] As explained above, under the Work Programme, all job search activities were outsourced to private, public and third-sector contractors on a payment-by-results basis. This gave rise to concerns, mentioned in Chapters 3 and 7, that contractors put pressure on staff to increase the number of sanctions in order to concentrate on easy-to-place customers and meet their performance targets. Work Programme staff were required to refer every missed appointment to the DWP to determine whether or not they should be sanctioned[16] and the more energetically they did this, the more claimants would be given a sanction.

As mentioned above, proportionality requires that the penalty should 'fit the crime', in the sense that less serious offences should receive less severe penalties while more serious offences should receive more severe ones. Benefit sanctions are variable but, while court fines can be set at whatever level, on a continuous scale, is thought to be commensurate with the severity of the offence and the culpability of the offender, benefit sanctions are limited to three (now four) levels (lowest, low, medium and high) that escalate with the severity of the offence and the number of prior sanctions (for details, see Chapter 3 above). This is clearly a much cruder form of proportionality than can be achieved with court fines. Proportionality also requires that the penalty should be neither more nor less severe than is appropriate and, in this regard, benefit sanctions clearly disproportionate. This is because the excessive penalties that are imposed are completely out of proportion to the minor misdemeanours that give rise to them.

Benefit sanctions are also like court fines in that they are disproportionately applied to people on low incomes. However, they differ from court fines since people who are fined can ask to pay by instalments, or in smaller amounts if they are already paying in instalments, or over a longer period or at a later date; while people who are sanctioned have their money stopped immediately and there is nothing they can do about

---

[15] According to an article by Patrick Wintour in *The Guardian*, an internal DWP Report (by Neil Couling) denied the existence of sanctions targets but accepted that action would be taken against Job Centres which imposed fewer sanctions than others. See Wintour (2013) and Couling (2013).

[16] On this, see Oakley (2014: 43–44).

this. When claimants in receipt of benefit are sanctioned, they lose their only or their main source of income.[17] As explained in Chapter 7, evidence of the effectiveness of sanctions in achieving their stated aim of getting claimants into sustainable paid employment is patchy and ambivalent.[18] At the same time, evidence points to the fact that many of those who are subject to benefit sanctions suffer considerable hardship, that sanctions can have a detrimental effect on health and well-being, and that those who are sanctioned often end up homeless, engage in street begging, use food banks and resort to crime.[19] The widespread and chronic hardship that results from the imposition of benefit sanctions indicate that they are excessive and that they are not proportionate to the minor offences that give rise to their imposition.[20]

Vulnerable claimants are most likely to be sanctioned and, despite the availability of hardship payments, many of those who are sanctioned experience considerable hardship, becoming homeless, engaging in street begging, using food banks and resorting to crime.[21] In spite of the existence of hardship payments, it is reasonable to conclude that benefit sanctions have a 'very severe' impact on claimants who are subject to them.

## IS LIKE BEING COMPARED WITH LIKE?

It should be acknowledged that some people may find it hard to accept that benefit sanctions can be compared with court fines because, while the latter are penalties that have to be paid out of a person's income or capital, the former involve the withdrawal of income that the person is (arguably) no longer entitled to and, comparing them does not involve comparing like with like. The position of those who are given a benefit sanction is, these critics might argue, more like that of applicants for social housing who may be turned down because they are deemed to be intentionally homeless or that of sitting tenants who may be evicted

---

[17] The minority of claimants who receive contribution-based JSA or non-means tested ESA may have other sources of income.

[18] The evidence is reviewed in Chapter 5 above.

[19] The evidence is likewise reviewed in Chapter 5 above.

[20] In 2013, the average amount of JSA in payment was just under £68.00–69.00 per week. Thus 4 weeks of sanctions were equivalent to a penalty of around £275.00 while 13 weeks of sanctions were equivalent to a penalty of about £900.00.

[21] See Chapter 5 above.

on the grounds that they have breached the tenancy conditions. There may be some merit in these arguments but to regard benefit sanctions in this way is ignore the fact that, like court fines, they affect the disposable income of those who are subject to them and their families.

There is an analogy between the comparison that is being made here and that between public expenditure (which refers to outflows of funds from the Exchequer for expenditure on benefits, services, infrastructure, debt interest and so on) and 'tax expenditure' (which refers to the numerous tax allowances, reliefs and deductions that have the effect of reducing inflows of funds into the Exchequer). Few people thought of comparing these aspects of government until, in a published lecture entitled 'The Social Division of Welfare', Richard Titmuss[22] made the argument that they were functionally equivalent.[23] The Royal Commission on the Taxation of Profits and Income noted, in 1955, that many of the tax reliefs built into the tax system 'amount[ed] in effect to a grant of public monies'[24] and similar points about the functional equivalence of public expenditure and tax expenditure have, over the years, been made by academics in a number of disciplines and countries, and by various national and international organisations. Today there are occasional skirmishes on the issue, but the linking of social spending and tax reliefs is now generally accepted by academics and public bodies in social policy, economics, political science, taxation and law.

## THE NATURE OF THE PENALTY

Benefit sanctions play an important part in what Wacquant[25] has called 'the new government of social insecurity' and illustrate the relevance for the UK of his claim that there has been a fundamental shift in recent decades in the USA away from liberal social policies towards a more punitive approach to managing the poor. Wacquant has pointed to the ways in which, in the USA, restrictive 'workfare' measures have been combined with expansive 'prisonfare' to produce an extremely punitive approach to poverty management.

[22] Titmuss (1965: 34–55).

[23] For a commentary on Titmuss' analysis, see Sinfield (1978).

[24] Royal Commission on the Taxation of Profits and Incomes (1955: 55).

[25] Wacquant (2009).

Although benefit sanctions are clearly punitive, they are also disciplinary, in a way that court fines are not. Within the criminal justice system, prisons are the embodiment of discipline in that, through surveillance, prison staff seek to control every aspect of the prisoner's life. Community disposals also have a disciplinary function, although they impose a less intrusive form of control. On the other hand, court fines have very little disciplinary content. They are, quite simply, monetary penalties—no more, no less. Benefit sanctions, on the other hand, do have a disciplinary function although, once they have been imposed, they are not associated with any form of surveillance. Unlike fines, benefit sanctions are ongoing and are intended to create what Foucault refers to as 'disciplined subjects',[26] i.e. claimants who 'actively seek employment', are prepared to take whatever low-paid and insecure jobs they are offered, and to meet the terms and conditions required for the receipt of benefit. In response to the resulting hardship, those who are sanctioned are expected to reflect on the experience and reform themselves. Unfortunately, the evidence reviewed in Chapter 6 does not indicate that sanctions are very effective.

Benefit sanctions can be seen to exemplify what, many years ago, Stanley Cohen referred to as 'the dispersal of control'.[27] Although Cohen was referring to the introduction of community disposals in the criminal justice system, his characterisation of this development in terms of 'widening the net' and 'thinning the mesh' applies equally well to the growth of benefit sanctions.

Flint has recently described the emergence of a 'centaur state' in which deregulation for social and economic elites is combined with an 'expansive and disciplinary mesh' thrown over marginalised groups to 'correct' their misconduct and 'inculcate their habituation to precarious low-wage labour, founded on self-blame and passivity'.[28] This 'mesh' involves the use of conditionality and, although conditionality within the benefits system is often seen as the 'archetypal' form of conditionality, conditional approaches are also used in other areas of social policy, for example in social housing, homelessness and anti-social behaviour policies. In all these areas, behavioural conditions are enforced through the use of penalties that reduce, suspend

---

[26] Foucault (1979: Chapter 1).

[27] Cohen (1979).

[28] Flint (2018).

**Table 9.2** Comparison of the salient characteristics of court fines and benefit sanctions

|  | *Court fines* | *Benefit sanctions* |
|---|---|---|
| How imposed? | Imposed judicially | Imposed bureaucratically |
| Relationship to adjudication | Precedes sanction (for those who plead not-guilty) | Follows sanction |
| Level of protection | Adequate | Inadequate before Mandatory reconsideration (MR), much worse afterwards |
| Immediate/delayed impact of sanctions | Time to pay (few pay immediately, many pay by instalments or by direct deduction from pay or benefits, some do not pay at all) | Take immediate effect |
| Duration | Imposed once, but can be paid over a period of time | Apply for extended periods, ranging from four weeks to three years |
| Socio-economic characteristics of sanctioned people | Mainly poor (many out of work) | Very poor (all out of work) |
| Impact on offenders | Moderate—some hardship | Very severe—extreme hardship |
| Proportionality | Could be more so | Could not be less so |
| Purpose | Punitive rather than disciplinary | Disciplinary as well as punitive |
| Relationship to justice | Relatively easy to make compatible—less needs to be done | More difficult to make compatible—more needs to be done |

or end access to benefits and services in an attempt to coerce those who are penalised to behave differently. Thus, although benefit sanctions, which are the subject of this book, are important in their own right, they also exemplify developments that are also encountered elsewhere.

The salient characteristics of court fines and benefit sanctions are compared in Table 9.2.

It is clear that benefit sanctions differ from court fines in numerous ways and that claimants who are sanctioned are given much less procedural protection than offenders who are fined. Benefit sanctions are not only disproportionate but also inconsistent with justice.

## CONCLUSION: WHAT CAN BE LEARNED FROM COMPARISONS WITH COURT FINES?

The comparison of benefit sanctions with court fines highlights many of the problems associated with benefit sanctions. Among these problems are the fact that, unlike court fines, benefit sanctions take immediate effect; they can only be challenged once they have been imposed; they apply for extended periods; they are disciplinary as well as punitive; they are disproportionate to the seriousness of the offence and they cannot be adjusted to take account of claimants' changing circumstances. Without wishing to suggest that the procedures for imposing fines on offenders in the courts provide a model that other types of monetary penalty should seek to emulate, the obstacles to reforming benefit sanctions to ensure that they have none of the features enumerated above, and that they are compatible with justice, are likely to be even greater than the obstacles to reforming court fines to reduce and, ideally, eliminate their unacceptable features.

## REFERENCES

Adler, M. (2008). The Idea of Proportionality in Dispute Resolution. *Journal of Social Welfare and Family Law, 30*(4), 309–322.

Ashworth, A. (2010). *Sentencing and Criminal Justice* (5th ed.). Cambridge: Cambridge University Press.

Cohen, S. (1979). The Punitive City: Notes on the Dispersal of Social Control. *Contemporary Crises, 3*, 339–363.

Comptroller and Auditor General's Office. (2006). *Fines Collection*. London: National Audit Office. Available at http://nao.org.uk/pn/05-061049.htm.

Comptroller and Auditor General's Office. (2007). *Improving Fines Collection Through Better Information on Defendants' Ability to Pay*. London: National Audit Office. Available at http://nao.org.uk/wp-content/uploads/2007/06/fines_collection.pdf.

Couling, N. (2013). *Conditionality and Sanctions: A Report to the Secretary of State for Work and Pensions*. London. Available at https://www.gov.uk/government/publications/conditionality-and-sanctions-a-report-to-the-secretary-of-state-for-work-and-pensions.

Flint, J. (2018). Encounters with the Centaur State: Advanced Urban Marginality and the Practices and Ethics if Welfare Sanctions Regimes. *Urban Studies*. Available online at https://www.urbanstudiesonline.com/mediacentre/news/encounters-with-the-centaur-state.

Foucault, M. (1979). *Discipline and Punish: The Birth of the Prison* (A. Sheridan, Trans.). New York: Vintage Books.

Garland, D. (2001). *The Culture of Control: Crime and the Social Order in Contemporary Society*. Oxford: Oxford University Press.

Larkin, P. (2007). The Criminalisation of Social Security Law: Towards a Punitive Welfare State. *Journal of Law and Society, 34*(3), 293–320.

Ministry of Justice. (2013). *Story of the Prison Population 1993–2012*. London: England and Wales.

Oakley, M. (2014). *Independent Review of the Operation of Jobseeker's Allowance Sanctions Validated by the Jobseekers Act 2013*. London: Department of Work and Pensions. Available at https://www.gov.uk/government/uploads/system/uploads/attachment_data/file/335144/jsa-sanctions-independent-review.pdf.

O'Malley, P. (2009). Theorizing Fines. *Punishment and Society, 11*(1), 67–83.

Royal Commission on the Taxation of Profits and Incomes (RCTPI). (1955). *Final Report*, Cmnd. 9474. London: HMSO.

Scottish Government. (2012). *Prison Statistics and Population Projections 2001–2012*. Edinburgh.

Sinfield, A. (1978). Analyses in the Social Division of Welfare. *Journal of Social Policy, 7*(2), 129–156.

Titmuss, R. (1965). *Essays on 'the Welfare State'* (2nd ed., pp. 34–55). London: Allen and Unwin.

von Hirsch, A., & Ashworth, A. (2005). *Proportionate Sentencing*. Oxford: Oxford University Press, especially Chapter 9 entitled 'Criteria for Proportionality: A Review'.

Wacquant, L. (2009). *Punishing the Poor: The Neoliberal Government of Social Insecurity*. Durham, NC and London: Duke University Press.

Walker, N. (1968). *Crime and Punishment in Britain*. Edinburgh: Edinburgh University Press.

Wintour, P. (2013, May 15). DWP Report Accepts Mistakes Made on Welfare Sanctions by Job Centres. *The Guardian*. Available at https://www.theguardian.com/society/2013/may/15/dwp-no-evidence-JobCentre-benefits-targets.

# CHAPTER 10

# Benefit Sanctions and the Rule of Law

There is an extensive literature on 'the rule of law', both by 'classical' writers[1] and by modern scholars.[2] However, few people have written as clearly on the subject as Tom Bingham, formerly Master of the Rolls, Lord Chief Justice of England and Wales, and Senior Law Lord in the UK Supreme Court, and his analysis will be used as a starting point.

## TOM BINGHAM ON 'THE RULE OF LAW'

According to Tom Bingham,[3] the 'rule of law' comprises eight principles. These are set out in Table 10.1.

This framework will now be used to determine whether benefit sanctions are compatible with the rule of law. Before doing so, what we take to be the salient characteristics of benefit sanctions from a rule of law perspective are summarised.

First, unlike fines that are imposed by the courts, benefit sanctions are not preceded by legal proceedings. There are, as we have explained in Chapter 7, established reconsideration and appeal procedures but, since there are no time limits, reconsideration can take a long time and

---

[1] See, for example, Locke (1689/1988), Dicey (1885/1979), Hayek (1944) and Hart (1961).

[2] See, for example, Raz (1979), MacCormick (2005) and Waldron (2005).

[3] Bingham (2010).

© The Author(s) 2018                                                  129
M. Adler, *Cruel, Inhuman or Degrading Treatment?*, Palgrave
Socio-Legal Studies, https://doi.org/10.1007/978-3-319-90356-9_10

**Table 10.1**  Eight principles of the rule of law

1. The law must be accessible and, so far as possible, intelligible, clear and predictable
2. Questions of legal right and liability should ordinarily be resolved by application of the law and not the exercise of discretion
3. The laws of the land should apply equally to all, save to the extent that objective differences justify differentiation
4. Ministers and public officials at all levels must exercise the powers conferred on them in good faith, fairly for the purpose for which the powers were conferred, without exceeding the limits of such powers and not unreasonably
5. The law must offer adequate protection of fundamental human rights
6. Means must be provided for resolving, without prohibitive cost or inordinate delay, bona fide civil disputes which the parties themselves are unable to resolve
7. Adjudicative procedures provided by the state should be fair
8. The rule of law requires compliance by the state of its obligations in international law as in national law

sanctions are not put on hold while claimants' cases are reviewed. The number of social security appeals to an independent tribunal increased by more than 600% between 2009 and 2013.[4] However, Mandatory Reconsideration (MR), which was introduced in 2013, was designed to choke this off and it appears to have done just that.

As explained in Chapter 7, until October 2013, when MR was introduced, claimants could either ask for the DWP's decision to impose a sanction to be reviewed, in which case, this would be undertaken by a different decision maker, or they could appeal directly to a tribunal. Now they must first request a second review or reconsideration. If the claimant disputes anything, the initial decision-maker will consider what they have to say, including any new evidence they present, and may change his/her decision at this point but, if not, and the claimant insists, the initial decision maker (not the claimant) can request a formal MR, which will be undertaken by a new, remotely-located Dispute Resolution Team (DRT), and only if they are turned down at this stage can the claimant appeal to a tribunal. It is hardly surprising that the number of appeals has plummeted.

This combination of internal review and external appeal procedures does not provide an acceptable level of legal protection for those who

---

[4] The number of JSA appeals increased from 6330 in 2009 to 34,022 in 2013. This represents a 540% increase over five years.

receive a benefit sanction. Because they are on benefit, they are among the poorest people in society and the sanctions they are given are extremely severe since they can deprive claimants of all their income for periods ranging from four weeks to three years. If the courts were to impose fines set at the level of the offender's disposable income, and to go on doing this for lengthy periods, there would be an outcry. Sanctions for a non-criminal offence that are set at 100% of the alleged offender's income and applied repeatedly are, clearly, totally lacking in proportionality.

As pointed out in Chapter 6, vulnerable claimants are most likely to be sanctioned and, despite the availability of hardship payments, many of those who are sanctioned experience considerable hardship. Anecdotal evidence suggests that many of them end up homeless, using food banks and resorting to crime. It is hard to see how these shortcomings could be rectified and it follows that benefit sanctions, as they have developed in the UK, are incompatible with justice, as well as ineffective and lacking in humanity.

The salient characteristics of benefit sanctions are set out in Table 10.2. Readers should note that this characterisation is taken from Table 9.2 above.

We now come to the question of whether benefit sanctions are compatible with the rule of law. My conclusion is that they are not. The consistency of benefit sanctions with each of Bingham's eight principles is discussed below.

**Table 10.2** The characteristics of benefit sanctions

| Characteristic | Benefit sanctions |
| --- | --- |
| How imposed? | Imposed administratively |
| Relationship to adjudication | Follows sanction |
| Level of protection | Inadequate before MR, much worse after MR |
| Severity of sanctions | Very severe indeed |
| Immediate/delayed impact of sanctions | Take immediate effect |
| Socio-economic characteristics of sanctioned people | Mainly very poor (all out of work) |
| Consequences of sanctions | Often extreme hardship |
| Proportionality | Could not be less so |
| Punishment for past behaviour/effects on future behaviour | Extremely punitive/effect on job seeking unproven |
| Relationship to justice | Very difficult to make compatible |

1. **Clarity of the law**: Although the Decision Makers' Guide[5] provides guidance for DWP staff who make decisions about benefits and pensions and helps them make decisions that are accurate and consistent, it is extremely complicated, containing 564 substantive paragraphs and 266 pages; and claimants have not been provided with any comparable account of the law that sets out when sanctions can be imposed and how they can be challenged. However, since October 2013, new jobseekers have been required to sign a 'Jobseekers' Agreement', which sets out what they need to do to receive state support. Although specifying what is expected of claimants is undoubtedly a step in the right direction, there must be very real doubts about whether the first principle is satisfied since 'good cause', 'just cause' and 'good reason' are not defined in legislation and have not been clarified by the Upper Tribunal or the courts. What claimants regard as 'good cause', 'just cause' and 'good reason' may well not be accepted as such by DWP decision-makers.[6]

2. **Determination of rights by law**: Most disputes involve the exercise of discretion and involve claimants asserting 'good cause', 'just cause' and 'good reason' for failing to meet administrative requirements that are rejected by DWP decision-makers. These disputes are handled internally while independent adjudication is only used in the very small number of cases that are appealed to a tribunal. Whether this would be regarded as sufficient to satisfy the second principle is an open question.

---

[5]  DWP decision-makers now use Advice for Decision Makers (ADM), instead of the DMG for decisions that involve Universal Credit, Personal Independence Payment, contribution-based Jobseeker's Allowance (JSA) and contribution-based Employment and Support Allowance (ESA).

[6]  In para 34204 of Chapter 34, the DMG points out that the concepts of 'good cause' and 'just cause' have been considered in case law, which makes it clear that they include facts that would probably have caused a reasonable person to act as the claimant did (reference is made to case 1 R(SB) 6/83). However, 'good reason' has not been considered in case law and it has been suggested that the 2012 Regulations deliberately replaced 'good cause' with 'good reason' to ensure that existing case law on 'good cause' did not automatically apply. Para 34205 points out that claimants will be given the opportunity to explain why they have not complied with requirements and that it is their responsibility to show 'good reason' for the failure and provide information and evidence as appropriate to explain why they have not complied.

3. **Equality of application**: Since the sanctions regime applies to everyone in receipt of means-tested benefits, the third principle might appear to be satisfied. However, sanction rates vary substantially between different Work Programme providers and, therefore, between Job Centres,[7] and there is considerable evidence that vulnerable claimants are more likely to be sanctioned than others.[8] According to the NAO, providers place different amounts of emphasis on sanctions as a tool for improving claimants' employment outcomes, and give different amounts of discretion to individual advisers.[9] It follows that there must be very real doubts about whether the third principle is satisfied.

4. **Reasonable exercise of discretion**: There is an accumulating body of evidence that sanctions are often applied unreasonably and for trivial administrative offences.[10] For example,

   - A man was sanctioned for missing appointment due to being at hospital with his partner, who had just had a stillborn child.
   - A man sanctioned for missing an appointment at the Job Centre on the day of his brother's unexpected death. He had tried to phone Jobcentre Plus to explain, but could not get through and left a message which was consequently not relayed to the appropriate person.
   - A young couple who had not received any letters regarding an appointment that they subsequently missed. Their address at the Department for Work and Pensions was wrongly recorded. They were left with no money for over a month.

5. **Respect for fundamental rights**: The attenuated arrangements for challenging the imposition of sanctions, which can leave people without any income for substantial periods of time indicate that the right to a fair trial, guaranteed under Article 6 of the ECHR,

---

[7] According to the Public Accounts Committee, some Work Programme providers make more than twice as many sanction referrals as other providers who support similar people in the same area, and that, between Job Centres, sanction rates also vary in ways that cannot be explained. See House of Commons Public Accounts Committee (2017: para 9).

[8] See Chapter 6 above.

[9] National Audit Office (2016: para 10).

[10] Butler (2015).

is inadequately protected. This suggests that the fifth principle is probably not satisfied.

6. **Access to justice**: Cost is not an issue since there are no financial barriers to challenging the DWP's decision to impose a sanction, but delay is, mainly because there are no time limits for the DWP to reconsider its decision. As a result, a claimant who wishes to challenge the imposition of a sanction may have to endure a long period without any income. Under MR, so many obstacles have been put in the way of getting to an independent tribunal that tribunal appeals have virtually disappeared; the right of appeal has, in effect, become a purely theoretical one. Lack of advice, caused by severe cuts to the funding of advice services, is also an issue although the demise of representation at tribunals is less of a problem both because there are fewer tribunal hearings and because tribunals now adopt a more inquisitorial mode of decision-making.[11] However, delays and the difficulty of accessing a tribunal suggest that the sixth principle is also probably not satisfied.

7. **Fair adjudication**: The adjudicative procedures provided by the state in tribunals that hear appeals are reasonably fair. However, the MR process which is, in effect, the last recourse for almost all claimants is clearly unfair because it is so one-sided, and it is manifestly not independent in the way that tribunals are. Thus, the difficulties experienced by claimants raise doubts about the fairness of the whole set of procedures for challenging the imposition of sanctions and the seventh principle is probably not satisfied.

8. **Compliance with international law**: Article 13 of the European Social Charter permits benefit sanctions but only if they do not deprive the person concerned of his/her means of subsistence, which is protected under Article 12. The situation in the UK is currently under review by the European Committee on Social Rights[12] but, on this ground alone, the fact that benefit sanctions deprive recipients of benefit of all their income for lengthy periods of time suggests that it is unlikely to satisfy the eighth principle.

---

[11] Adler (2009).

[12] European Social Charter, European Committee of Social Rights 2013 (2014) Conclusions XX–2, United Kingdom—Article 13, 29 January. For a commentary, see Cashman (2014).

## CONCLUSION: DO BENEFIT SANCTIONS CONFORM WITH THE RULE OF LAW?

Using Tom Bingham's eight 'rule of law' principles as a template, the number of counts on which the current sanctions regime in the UK appears not to satisfy these principles indicates that there are serious questions about its legality, in addition to the serious questions about its effectiveness, humanity and injustice. Another characterisation of the rule of law would, no doubt, produce different conclusions but there is no doubt that, from a rule of law perspective, there is something very wrong with the current sanctions regime.

## REFERENCES

Adler, M. (2009, March). Tribunals Ain't What They Used to Be. *Adjust Newsletter*. Available at http://www.ajtc.gov.uk/adjust/09_03.htm.

Bingham, T. (2010). *The Rule of Law*. London: Allen Lane.

Butler, P. (2015, March 24). Benefit Sanctions: The 10 Trivial Breaches and Administrative Errors. *The Guardian*. Available at https://www.the-guardian.com/society/2015/mar/24/benefit-sanctions-trivial-breaches-and-administrative-errors.

Cashman, D. (2014). Not Reaping the Benefits: The United Kingdom's Continuing Violation of Article 12(1) of the European Social Charter. *Oxford Human Rights Law Blog*. Available at http://ohrh.law.ox.ac.uk/not-reaping-the-benefits-the-united-kingdoms-continuing-violation-of-article-12%C2%A71-of-the-european-social-charter/.

Dicey, A. V. (1885/1979). *Introduction to the Study of the Law of the Constitution*. London: Palgrave Macmillan.

Hart, H. L. A. (1961/1972). *The Concept of Law*. Oxford: Oxford University Press.

Hayek, F. A. (1944). *The Road to Serfdom*. London: Routledge.

House of Commons Public Accounts Committee. (2017, February 21). *Benefit Sanctions*, HC 775, 42nd Report of Session 2016–2017. Available at https://publications.parliament.uk/pa/cm201617/cmselect/cmpubacc/775/775.pdf.

Locke, J. (1689/1988). *Two Treatises of Government*. Cambridge Texts in the History of Political Thought. Cambridge: Cambridge University Press.

MacCormick, N. (2005). *Rhetoric and the Rule of Law: A Theory of Legal Reasoning*. Oxford: Oxford University Press.

National Audit Office. (2016, November 17). *Benefit Sanctions: Detailed Methodology*. London: National Audit Office. Available at https://www. nao.org.uk/wp-content/uploads/2016/11/Benefit-sanctions-detailed-methodology.pdf.

Raz, J. (1979). The Rule of Law and Its Virtues. In *The Authority of Law: Essays on Law and Morality*. Oxford: Oxford University Press.

Waldron, J. (2005). Is the Rule of Law an Essentially Contested Concept? In R. Bellamy (Ed.), *The Rule of Law and the Separation of Powers*. Farnham: Ashgate.

# CHAPTER 11

# What, if anything, can be done about Benefit Sanctions?

The main aim of conditionality in social security, i.e. of increased job search requirements and more severe benefit sanctions, is to get those on benefit into sustainable paid employment. However, as this book has sought to demonstrate, the solution has not worked and has itself become a problem. In this sense it is like mass incarceration in the USA. The original problem was crime to which imprisonment was seen to be the solution. Eventually, the excessive, disproportionate, unfair, ineffective and counter-productive character of mass incarceration became apparent and, for many critics, it became the problem. In this case, welfare dependency, fiddling and abuse were perceived to be the problem and benefit sanctions the solution, but things have gone too far and, as demonstrated in this book, sanctions have been used disproportionately and applied harshly and arbitrarily. Thus, they should now be seen as a problem in need of a solution.

In recent years, as concern with benefit sanctions has mounted, there have been several inquiries into the operation and impact of benefit sanctions by official bodies. We focus in this chapter on three recent reports, by the House of Commons Work and Pensions Select Committee in 2015, by the National Audit Office in 2016, and by the House of Commons Public Accounts Select Committee in 2017. Ten proposals for addressing the injustice associated with benefit sanctions and ameliorating the hardship they cause are then outlined, and the possibility of incorporating the European Social Charter into legislation, in much the same way that the European Convention on Human Rights has been

© The Author(s) 2018    137
M. Adler, *Cruel, Inhuman or Degrading Treatment?*, Palgrave
Socio-Legal Studies, https://doi.org/10.1007/978-3-319-90356-9_11

incorporated in the Human Rights Act 1998, floated since this would provide greater legal protection for those who are sanctioned. In the event that none of these measures are taken up, the chapter concludes by considering an alternative to a social security system based on conditionality, namely a basic income scheme.

## HOUSE OF COMMONS WORK AND PENSIONS SELECT COMMITTEE REPORT[1]

In its report, published in March 2015, the House of Commons Work and Pensions Committee repeated the call in its previous report for a comprehensive, independent review of benefit sanctions and for a serious attempt to resolve the conflicting demands on claimants made by Jobcentre Plus and Work Programme staff that would enable them to take a common-sense view on 'good reasons' for non-compliance with Departmental expectations. The Committee concluded that there was no evidence to support the longer sanction periods that were introduced in October 2012 and recommended the piloting of pre-sanction written warnings and non-financial sanctions.

In its response to the report, the DWP rejected all the recommendations that would have thrown further light on the problems of the system, namely: a comprehensive independent review, a specific review of ESA sanctioning, an exploration of alternatives to financial sanctions (other than possibly for ESA claimants), an evaluation of the lengthening of sanctions in 2012, an evaluation of the Claimant Commitment, monitoring the destinations of sanctioned claimants, and reform of the legislative framework. It also rejected the recommendation that all claimants should be allowed to apply for a hardship payment from day one of a sanction, rather than waiting for two weeks, and gave up on its attempts to prevent the wrongful cancellation of housing benefit for JSA claimants who are sanctioned. Sanctioned claimants were often not informed that their housing benefit had been cancelled and only became aware of this when their landlord told them they were hundreds of pounds in rent arrears.[2]

---

[1]   House of Commons Work and Pensions Committee (2015).

[2]   In September 2015, the DWP belatedly issued guidance making it clear that claimants who are in receipt of passported housing benefit should continue to receive it without interruption when a sanction is applied.

## THE NATIONAL AUDIT OFFICE REPORT[3]

The NAO report, published in November 2016, set out to assess whether the DWP was achieving value for money in its administration of benefit sanctions. It concluded that this was difficult to assess because the Department has so little evidence of how people respond to the threat or the imposition of sanctions.[4] It noted that the government had increased the scope and severity of sanctions but expressed concern that the impact of this change had not been monitored and drew attention to the extent of variation between Job Centres and between Work Programme providers. Its recommendations were related to its findings. Thus, it recommended that the Department should measure the impact of sanctions on employment and on the demand for other services; that it should enhance its management information systems and its collection of statistical data, and use them to improve its decision making; and that it should explore ways of reducing variations among and between Job Centres and providers.

## HOUSE OF COMMONS PUBLIC ACCOUNTS COMMITTEE REPORT[5]

Following on from the NAO Report, the Public Accounts Committee (PAC) recommended in its report, published in February 2017, that the DWP should undertake a trial of warnings for the first sanctionable offence, monitor variations in referrals from Job Centres and Work Programme providers and the take-up of hardship payments; improve its understanding of the impact of sanctions on claimants and their costs to government, investigate the impact of sanctions on employment and earnings; and improve its collection of statistical data as recommended by the UK Statistics Authority.

---

[3]  Comptroller and Auditor General (2016).

[4]  This cannot be an accident or an oversight because the DWP's failure to collect and analyse statistical data on the impact of benefit sanctions has been pointed out so often. The absence of information is clearly intended and reflects the ideological commitment of successive Labour, Coalition and Conservative Governments to the principle of conditionality.

[5]  House of Commons Public Accounts Committee (2017).

Most of the recommendations in the three reports are very sensible, but it cannot really be said that they get to the heart of the problem. They do not directly challenge the need for benefit sanctions and are designed to make the administration of benefit sanctions more consistent, more effective and more humane. Most of them involve tinkering around at the edges. If they were implemented, they would undoubtedly improve the operation of benefit sanctions. However, a more 'root and branch' consideration of the operation of benefit sanctions is called for.

## WHAT COULD BE DONE?

### *Action Research*

There is a strong case for conducting some action research to find out what works and what does not, i.e. how to keep claimants engaged with the world of work and prevent them from dropping out. One controversial possibility would involve commissioning the Behavioural Insights Team,[6] which redesigns public services by drawing on ideas from the behavioural sciences. Its approach is an empirical one: it tests and trials ideas before they are scaled up and, in this way, attempts to identify what works and (importantly) what does not work.

### *Reforms to Benefit Sanctions*

There are numerous ways in which the injustice associated with benefit sanctions and the suffering they cause could be ameliorated. These aims could be accomplished, for example, by:

- limiting the circumstances in which sanctions can be imposed—so that they are only imposed for what are deemed to be serious breaches of conditions;

---

[6] The Behavioural Insights Team (BIT) is a social purpose company, which is jointly owned by the UK Government; the National Endowment for Science, Technology and the Arts (NESTA) and its employees. BIT started life inside 10 Downing Street as a government institution dedicated to the application of the behavioural sciences to public policy. Its objectives are:
  - to make public services more cost-effective and easier for citizens to use;
  - to improve outcomes by introducing a more realistic model of human behaviour to policy; and wherever possible, and
  - to enable people to make 'better choices for themselves'.

- minimising or preventing altogether the imposition of sanctions on particularly deprived or vulnerable people—e.g. single parents, people with mental or physical illness or disabilities, homeless people or those in precarious housing circumstances etc.
- reducing the severity of sanctions—so that, instead of depriving claimants of all their benefit, claimants are deprived of a fixed amount or a proportion of their benefit; and that the minimum and maximum duration of sanctions is reduced from four weeks to, say, one week (minimum) and from 156 weeks to, say, four weeks (maximum);
- developing non-financial penalties, which might include carrying out unpaid work, such as cleaning, removing graffiti, gardening for old people, painting and decorating etc., that could replace or be offered as an alternative to financial penalties[7];
- separating the two sides of conditionality so that all claimants who are sanctioned, and lose their benefit, continue to have contact with the Job Centre and are given help with job search and training—currently, they may continue to have contact with the Job Centre but only if they sign on;
- adopting a more generous conception of 'good cause', so that what counts as 'good cause' takes all the relevant circumstances into account[8];
- issuing claimants with a warning before imposing a sanction—as recommended in each of the recent reports on benefit sanctions, i.e. by the House of Commons Work and Pensions Committee, the National Audit Office and the House of Commons Public Accounts Committee;
- giving claimants an opportunity to attend a hearing before a sanction is imposed—which would promote legality at the expense of bureaucracy and make bureaucratic decision makers subject to the rule of law;
- presenting claimants with the evidence on which the case for imposing sanctions is based and allowing them to challenge it—this

---

[7] It is recognised that these non-financial penalties assume that placements are available, and claimants are willing to take part.

[8] Warren (2006) compares the approach that used to be taken, in which decision-makers were expected to apply principles established in case law, with the approach that is now taken, in which they are required to apply an elaborate set of bureaucratic rules to the facts of the case. It is the old approach that is being suggested here.

would also promote legality at the expense of bureaucracy (inflexible application of rules and regulations) and discretion (by Work Coaches and DWP staff) and, almost certainly, lead to improved decision-making;

- allowing claimants to appeal directly to a tribunal when sanctions are imposed—since the 'success rate' of appealing to a tribunal is so much higher than the 'success rate' for Mandatory Reconsideration,[9] this would result in many more incorrect or inappropriate sanction decisions being overturned.

These 10 suggestions involve imposing constraints on the 'structural' and 'epistemic' aspects of the discretion exercised by DWP decision-makers.[10] Thus, the first five suggestions are structural in that they would curtail the scope and extent of discretion while the second five are epistemic in that they would involve enhancing the claimant's role in the decision to impose a sanction with a view to improving the quality of that decision.

### *Other Reforms*

Another proposal that merits serious consideration involves giving constitutional status to ESC rights in the same way as it has been given to ECHR rights; imposing a duty on government and parliament to comply with international standards (and allowing the courts to make declarations of incompatibility); and/or imposing a duty on them to 'have due regard' to the rights contained in these international treaties. This would make the UK Government more accountable to international treaties it has ratified and give greater protection to economic and social rights. However, in light of the opt-out secured for the UK and Poland from Protocol 7 of the Lisbon Treaty[11] and the fact that Tony Blair, who was then Prime Minster, made it absolutely clear that the UK would 'not accept a treaty that allows the charter of fundamental rights to change UK law in any

---

[9]   See Chapter 8 above.

[10]   This distinction is based on Molander (2016). 'Structural' discretion refers to the scope and extent of discretion while 'epistemic' discretion refers to the quality of discretionary decisions and the reasoning associated with them.

[11]   Barnard (2008).

way',[12] and in light of the fact that the UK voted to leave the EU in the European Referendum in 2016, this is probably wishful thinking.

### Prospects for Change

Unfortunately, because, until now, successive governments have been so committed to the principle of conditionality in the delivery of social security, and have clearly believed, as an article of faith, in the efficacy of benefit sanctions, they have been largely immune to any serious proposals for reform. This commitment reached its apotheosis during the five years of the Coalition Government when Iain Duncan Smith was Secretary of State for Work and Welfare.[13] Iain Duncan Smith increased the scope and severity of benefit sanctions in 2012 and refused to monitor their effectiveness or their impact on claimants' well-being. However, he lost his job in 2015 and, while none of his seemingly more pragmatic successors[14] has criticised or sought to reform the policy, none of them appears to have the same ideological commitment to it.

With Iain Duncan Smith no longer in office, the Conservative Government no longer having a majority in parliament and having to respond to a resurgent Labour Party, which is now committed to scrapping 'punitive sanctions',[15] it is possible that the government may become more receptive to reform proposals like those listed above in the future. The much lower unemployment rate, the much-reduced number of unemployed claimants and the considerably smaller number of benefit sanctions imposed by the DWP may facilitate their reform. If not, and if the continuing injustice to the smaller number of people who are subject to benefit sanctions is seen to warrant it, consideration will need to be given to devising a system of support for the unemployed that does not entail the use of sanctions.

---

[12] Reported in the House of Commons European Scrutiny Committee's 35th Report of Session 2006–2007, HC 1014, para 52.

[13] Margaret Hodge, who was Chair of the House of Commons Public Accounts Committee throughout this period, refers to his 'ideological conviction' in privatising the Work Programme but could equally well have been referring to his belief in the efficacy of benefit sanctions and his indifference to the hardship they cause. See Hodge (2016).

[14] Stephen Crabb, Damian Green, David Gauke and Esther McVey.

[15] Labour Party (2017) *Election Manifesto: Social Security*, available at https://labour.org.uk/manifesto/social-security/.

## *Alternatives to Benefit Sanctions*

In a recent contribution, Stuart White claims that there are two arguments for conditionality[16]: a paternalist argument based on the belief that conditionality is good for the recipient of benefits, and a fairness argument based on the argument that it is fair to others.[17] According to the principle of reciprocity, each of us owes our society, as a matter of fairness, a reasonably productive contribution in return for receiving a sufficiently fair share of the benefits generated by others but this requires a set of external conditions to be met. He goes on to suggest that these conditions comprise the existence of due process and dignity rights, fair taxation of asset income, recognition and support for care work, fair equality of opportunity and fair rewards, and to argue that, in the UK, they are currently not met.

Although a more restricted view of the justificatory conditions that need to be met is taken here, it is a central contention of this book that, in terms of their severity and duration, the fact that they take immediate effect, the suffering they impose on claimants, their limited effectiveness in getting claimants into employment, and the difficulties associated with challenging them, it is unlikely that the justificatory conditions are currently being met. It follows that sanctions as they exist today can not be justified. If it proves impossible through a set of reforms, such as those that listed above, to reform the sanctions regime so that the necessary justificatory conditions are met, then an alternative set of arrangement that does not depend on reciprocity or on conditionality needs to be considered. It is in this context that Stuart White considers the argument for an unconditional minimum income (UMI), otherwise known as Basic Income (BI). According to him,

> The basic idea is that, since the background conditions ... are not satisfied and there is a serious risk that they will not be satisfied in the future, we should proceed on the assumption that conditionality is likely to be unjust for the foreseeable future and that we should therefore seek to move away from it. Introducing a full BI, set at a level sufficient to meet a standard set

---

[16] White (2017).

[17] Anders Molander and Gaute Torsvik (2015) argue that there are four arguments for mandatory activation. In addition to the two arguments by Stuart White, they refer to efficiency (the gains from mandatory activation outweigh the costs) and sustainability (mandatory activation helps to sustain the welfare state).

of basic needs, with additional benefits to cover the higher living costs of sick and disabled people, is the ideal. However, even a partial BI, set at a level below this, would go some way towards reducing the stakes of unjust conditionality.[18]

One criticism of this argument is that it may be even more difficult to introduce a full BI, even a partial BI for the unemployed, than it would be to reform the current sanctions regime. However, although it certainly would not be easy to introduce BI, it would not be impossible.[19] Another criticism is that BI is 'a wasteful distraction from more practical methods', such as introducing real improvements to social security and a guarantee of full employment, for tackling poverty and inequality and ensuring that everyone has a right to an adequate income.[20] Reforming benefit sanctions may turn out to be the best option.

## Conclusion: Is There a Way Forward

Numerous policies could be adopted to improve the effectiveness of benefit sanctions and reduce the hardship they cause, which drives many of its victims into destitution. Whether any of them will be implemented is an open question. If any of these policies were to be adopted in the future, the question would arise of why they had not been adopted in the past. For as long as a centrist government is in power, it is unlikely that any of the reforms will be implemented. However, there is now a very real prospect that a radical government, which is less committed to the principle of conditionality, might be elected in the foreseeable future. The Green Party[21] committed itself to piloting a universal basic income

---

[18]  White (2017: 191).

[19]  In Finland, under a two-year, nationwide pilot scheme, which began on 1 January 2017, 2000 unemployed people between the ages of 25 and 58 are being given a guaranteed sum of €560 (£500) a month for two years. It replaces their unemployment benefit and they will continue to receive it if they find work. The government hopes it will encourage the unemployed to take on part-time work without worrying about losing their benefits and, by uncoupling work and social security, benefit sanctions for failing to look for work or take up offers of work will become a thing of the past. See Chakrabortty (2017).

[20]  See Piachaud (2016).

[21]  Bartley (2017).

scheme in its 2017 election manifesto and the Labour Party has recently set up a 'working group' to investigate the feasibility of a basic income scheme and to report back on its conclusions before the next general election.[22] If radical alternatives to a social security system that imposes extensive job search requirements and severe benefit sanctions are being seriously considered, the prospects for less radical but nonetheless significant reforms must be better than has hitherto been the case.

## References

Barnard C. (2008). The 'Opt-Out' for the UK and Poland from the Charter of Fundamental Rights: Triumph of Rhetoric over Reality? In S. Griller & J. Ziller (Eds.), *The Lisbon Treaty. Schriftenreihe der Österreichischen Gesellschaft für Europaforschung*. European Community Studies Association of Austria Publication Series (Vol. 11). Vienna: Springer.

Bartley, J. (2017, 2 June). The Greens Endorse a Universal Basic Income. Others Need to Follow. *The Guardian*.

Chakrabortty, A. (2017, October 31). A Basic Income for Everyone: Yes, Finland Shows It Really Can Work. *The Guardian*. Available at https://www.theguardian.com/commentisfree/2017/oct/31/finland-universal-basic-income.

Comptroller and Auditor General. (2016). *Benefit Sanctions*, HC 628, Session 2016–17. London: National Audit Office. Available at https://www.nao.org.uk/wp-content/uploads/2016/11/Benefit-sanctions.pdf.

Cowburn, A. (2017, February 5). Labour has Set Up a 'Working Group' to Investigate the Radical Idea of a Basic Income and will Report Back on its Conclusions before the next General Election, John McDonnell has said. *The Independent*.

Hodge, M. (2016). *Called to Account*. London: Abacus.

House of Commons Public Accounts Committee. (2017, February 21). *Benefit Sanctions*, HC 775, 42nd Report of Session 2016–2017. Available at https://publications.parliament.uk/pa/cm201617/cmselect/cmpubacc/775/775.pdf.

---

[22] In an interview with *The Independent*, John McDonnell, the Shadow Chancellor, who will be publishing the report together with one of his economic advisers, Guy Standing, a founder member of the Basic Income European Network, appeared to signal his personal desire to include basic income in the Labour Party's manifesto for the next general election. See Cowburn (2017).

House of Commons Work and Pensions Committee. (2015, March 24). *Benefit Sanctions Policy Beyond the Oakley Review*, HC 214, 5th Report of Session 2014–2015. Available at https://publications.parliament.uk/pa/cm201415/cmselect/cmworpen/814/814.pdf.

Labour Party. (2017). *Election Manifesto: Social Security*. Available at https://labour.org.uk/manifesto/social-security/.

Molander, A. (2016). *Discretion in the Welfare State*. London and New York: Routledge.

Molander, A., & Torsvik, G. (2015). Getting People into Work: What, (if Anything) Can Justify Mandatory Activation of Welfare Recipients? *Journal of Applied Philosophy, 32*(4), 373–392.

Piachaud, D. (2016, November). *Citizen's Income: Rights and Wrongs* (CASE/200). Centre for Analysis of Social Exclusion, London School of Economics.

Warren, N. (2006). The Adjudication Gap: A Discussion Document. *Journal of Social Security Law, 13*(2), 110–118.

White, S. (2017). Should a Minimum Income Be Unconditional? In S. C. Matteucci & S. Halliday (Eds.), *Social Rights in Europe in an Age of Austerity* (pp. 181–196). London and New York: Routledge.

# CHAPTER 12

# Conclusion

When benefit sanctions were at their peak, they constituted a modern Leviathan, a veritable monster that preyed on huge numbers of claimants and made their lives a misery.[1] Although the number of benefit sanctions that are imposed on claimants in the UK has, thankfully, declined since their peak of over 1 million a year in 2013, their characteristic features are unchanged. The same means for punishing and disciplining the poor that were in place when unemployment was at its peak are still in place today, in spite of the fact that unemployment has fallen.

The account of benefit sanctions given in this book cannot claim to be neutral or 'value free'. The underlying premise is that human rights include the right to a social minimum, i.e. to possess the basic necessities of life that enable people to live autonomous lives and maintain their self-respect. These human rights are universal and apply across the board to everyone, including people like 'terrorists' and people with 'extremist' opinions, asylum seekers, prisoners, 'benefit cheats' and 'welfare tourists', all of whom are frequently regarded as 'outsiders' who do not belong to civil society and who cannot claim the rights that apply to those who are members. This list of social outcasts includes those who are subject to benefit sanctions, who receive no income for extended periods, who often experience great hardship and who face the prospect of homelessness and a life on the streets. However, as explained in the introduction,

---

[1] Adler (2016).

© The Author(s) 2018            149
M. Adler, *Cruel, Inhuman or Degrading Treatment?*, Palgrave
Socio-Legal Studies, https://doi.org/10.1007/978-3-319-90356-9_12

the primary aim of this book is to determine whether the benefit sanctions regime in the UK is acceptable as it stands, whether it is capable of being reformed or whether it needs to be replaced. The book presents the empirical evidence on which such a judgment should be based.

With the demise of capital punishment, transportation and most forms of corporal punishment, imprisonment is now the most severe form of punishment in the UK. It deprives people of their liberty, the enjoyment of their personal possessions, normal sexual relationships and personal autonomy, and puts them at considerable risk of violence from fellow inmates.[2] Whether it constitutes 'cruel, inhuman or degrading treatment' depends on whether the deprivation it entails is more severe than it needs to be to secure its ends: protecting the public by removing offenders from communities (incapacitation); punishing the offender by delivering retribution in an appropriate but proportionate way where a serious crime has been committed; serving as a deterrent to the offender and/or to others; and rehabilitating the offender.

As a penalty imposed by the state, benefit sanctions are obviously not as extreme as incarceration. Moreover, they make fewer headlines than the hounding of refugees and asylum seekers by the Home Office, which entails persecution and deprives them, or threatens to deprive them, of their rights to enter or remain in the UK. However, that does not exonerate the persistent, insensitive, uncaring and relentless harassment by the DWP of those who fail to meet the requirements of conditionality in social security.

This book set out to ask whether the UK benefit sanctions regime constitutes 'cruel', 'inhuman' or 'degrading' treatment? In answering this question, the evidence relating to their **efficiency** in getting unemployed, sick and disabled claimants back into paid employment, their **impact** on claimants' well-being, and the **justice** involved both in administering and challenging benefit sanctions and in the relationship between the behaviour that gives rise to the penalty and the penalty itself, needs to be considered. The evidence presented in the book indicates that sanctions fail on all three counts in that they are inefficient, cause great suffering and are unjust.

Broadly speaking, it is contended here that there is widespread agreement in society that the term **'cruel'** is appropriate when the treatment

---

[2]   Sykes (1958/2007).

or punishment of an individual causes greater suffering than is necessary, proportionate or appropriate[3]; treatment or punishment can be described as '**inhuman**' if no human being could or should have to put up with it[4]; and as '**degrading**' if it is experienced, by the victim, or by observers, as humiliating or undermining the person's dignity.[5] Although the tests are very stringent, the conclusion of this book is that benefit sanctions in the UK are actually more cruel, more inhuman and more degrading than they need to be.

Some readers will, no doubt, take the view that it is wrong to attach any conditions to the receipt of benefits for those who are out of work because everyone should be entitled to a basic minimum income from the state. They will regard the hardship that is undoubtedly associated with benefit sanctions as pointless and gratuitous and therefore as unjustified and unacceptable. Others will take the view that, because rights entail responsibilities, it is appropriate for the state to attach conditions to the receipt of benefits for those who are not in work. The question then arises as to whether the hardship that is associated with benefit sanctions can be justified in terms of their effectiveness in persuading those on benefit to take up sustainable paid employment. For these readers, there will be a trade-off between hardship and effectiveness. If benefit sanctions were effective, they might consider that the hardship is a price worth paying.[6] However, that would leave justice, which is arguably the most important criterion, out of the equation. In terms of justice, the UK benefit sanctions regime undoubtedly fails the test.

## References

Adler, M. (2016). The New Leviathan: Benefit Sanctions in the 21st Century. *Journal of Law and Society, 43*(2), 195–227.

Sykes, G. (1958/2007). *The Society of Captives: A Study of a Maximum-Security Prison.* Princeton, NJ: Princeton University Press.

Waldron, J. (2008). *Cruel, Inhuman, and Degrading Treatment: The Words Themselves* (New York University Public Law and Legal Theory Working Papers, No. 98). Available at http://lsr.nellco.org/nyu_plltwp/98.

[3] Waldron (2008: 28).

[4] Ibid.: 31.

[5] Ibid.: 39–40.

[6] If sanctions are not effective, as seems to be the case, the hardship they undoubtedly cause will have been in vain.

# BIBLIOGRAPHY

Abercrombie, N., & Turner, B. S. (1978). The Dominant Ideology Thesis. *British Journal of Sociology, 29*(2), 149–170.

Adler, M. (2004). Combining Welfare-to-Work Measures with Tax Credits: A New Hybrid Approach to Social Security. *International Social Security Review, 57*(2), 87–106.

Adler, M. (2006). Fairness in Context. *Journal of Law and Society, 33*(4), 615–638.

Adler, M. (2008a). The Idea of Proportionality in Dispute Resolution. *Journal of Social Welfare and Family Law, 30*(4), 309–322.

Adler, M. (2008b). The Justice Implications of Activation Policies in the UK. In S. Stendahl, T. Erhag, & S. Devetzi (Eds.), *A European Work-First Welfare State*. Gothenburg: Centre for European Research, University of Gothenburg.

Adler, M. (2009, March). Tribunals Ain't What They Used to Be. *Adjust Newsletter*. Available at http://www.ajtc.gov.uk/adjust/09_03.htm.

Adler, M. (2010). Understanding and Analysing Administrative Justice. In M. Adler (Ed.), *Administrative Justice in Context*. Oxford: Hart Publishing.

Adler, M. (2012). The Rise and Fall of Administrative Justice—A Cautionary Tale. *Socio-Legal Review, 8*(2), 28–54.

Adler, M. (2013). Conditionality, Sanctions and the Effective Absence of Redress in the British "New Deal" Programs. In E. Z. Brodkin & G. Marston (Eds.), *Work and the Welfare State: The Politics and Management of Policy Change* (pp. 229–248). Washington, DC: Georgetown University Press; Copenhagen: DJØF.

Adler, M. (2016). The New Leviathan: Benefit Sanctions in the 21st Century. *Journal of Law and Society, 43*(2), 195–227.

© The Editor(s) (if applicable) and The Author(s) 2018
M. Adler, *Cruel, Inhuman or Degrading Treatment?*, Palgrave
Socio-Legal Studies, https://doi.org/10.1007/978-3-319-90356-9

Adler, M., & Terum, L. I. (2018). Austerity, Conditionality and Litigation in Six European Countries. In S. C. Matteucci & S. Halliday (Eds.), *Social Rights in an Age of Austerity: European Perspectives* (pp. 147–177). London: Routledge.

Ashworth, A. (2010). *Sentencing and Criminal Justice* (5th ed.). Cambridge: Cambridge University Press.

Baldwin, J., Wikeley, N., & Young, R. (1992). *Judging Social Security Claims*. Oxford: Clarendon Press.

Barnard C. (2008). The 'Opt-Out' for the UK and Poland from the Charter of Fundamental Rights: Triumph of Rhetoric over Reality? In S. Griller & J. Ziller (Eds.), *The Lisbon Treaty. Schriftenreihe der Österreichischen Gesellschaft für Europaforschung*. European Community Studies Association of Austria Publication Series (Vol. 11). Vienna: Springer.

Bartley, J. (2017, 2 June). The Greens Endorse a Universal Basic Income. Others Need to Follow. *The Guardian*.

Baumberg, B. (2014). Benefits and the Cost of Living. Pressures on the Cost of Living and Attitudes to Benefit Claiming. In *British Social Attitudes 31*. Available at http://www.bsa.natcen.ac.uk/media/38191/bsa31_benefits_and_the_cost_of_living.pdf.

Beveridge, W. (1942). *Social Insurance and Allied Services (Beveridge Report)*, Cmd. 6404. London: HMSO.

Bingham, T. (2010). *The Rule of Law*. London: Allen Lane.

Bourdieu, P. (1990). *The Logic of Practice*. Cambridge: Polity Press.

Boyle, K., & Hughes, E. (2018). Identifying Routes to Remedy for Violations of Economic, Social and Cultural Rights. *International Journal of Human Rights, 22*(1), 43–69.

Brodkin, E. Z. (2013). Work and the Welfare State. In E. Z. Brodkin & G. Marston (Eds.), *Work and the Welfare State: The Politics and Management of Policy Change*. Washington, DC: Georgetown University Press; Copenhagen: DJØF.

Brodkin, E. Z., & Marston, G. (Eds.). (2013). *Work and the Welfare State: The Politics and Management of Policy Change*. Washington, DC: Georgetown University Press; Copenhagen: DJØF.

Butler, P. (2015, March 24). Benefit Sanctions: The 10 Trivial Breaches and Administrative Errors. *The Guardian*. Available at https://www.theguardian.com/society/2015/mar/24/benefit-sanctions-trivial-breaches-and-administrative-errors.

Carter, E., & Whitworth, A. (2015). Creaming and Parking in Quasi-marketised Welfare-to-Work Schemes: Designed-Out of or Designed-In to the UK Work Programme? *Journal of Social Policy, 44*(2), 277–296.

Cashman, D. (2014). Not Reaping the Benefits: The United Kingdom's Continuing Violation of Article 12(1) of the European Social Charter.

*Oxford Human Rights Law Blog*. Available at http://ohrh.law.ox.ac.uk/not-reaping-the-benefits-the-united-kingdoms-continuing-violation-of-article-12%C2%A71-of-the-european-social-charter/.

Chakrabortty, A. (2017, October 31). A Basic Income for Everyone: Yes, Finland Shows It Really Can Work. *The Guardian*. Available at https://www.theguardian.com/commentisfree/2017/oct/31/finland-universal-basic-income.

Christensen, T., & Lægrid, P. (2007). The Whole-of-Government Approach to Public Sector Reform. *Public Administration Review, 67*(6), 1059–1066.

Citizens Advice Scotland. (2012). *Voices from the Frontline: JSA Sanctions*. Edinburgh. Available at https://www.cas.org.uk/publications/voices-frontline-jsa-sanctions.

Clasen, J., & Clegg, D. (2007). Levels and Levers of Conditionality: Measuring Change within Welfare States. In J. Clasen & N. A. Siegal (Eds.), *Investigating Welfare State Change: The 'Dependent Variable Problem' in Comparative Analysis* (pp. 166–197). Cheltenham: Edward Elgar.

Cohen, S. (1979). The Punitive City: Notes on the Dispersal of Social Control. *Contemporary Crises, 3*, 339–363.

Comptroller and Auditor General's Office. (2006). *Fines Collection*. London: National Audit Office. Available at http://nao.org.uk/pn/05-061049.htm.

Comptroller and Auditor General's Office. (2007). *Improving Fines Collection Through Better Information on Defendants' Ability to Pay*. London: National Audit Office. Available at http://nao.org.uk/wp-content/uploads/2007/06/fines_collection.pdf.

Comptroller and Auditor General. (2016). *Benefit Sanctions*, HC 628, Session 2016–17. London: National Audit Office. Available at https://www.nao.org.uk/wp-content/uploads/2016/11/Benefit-sanctions.pdf.

Couling, N. (2013). *Conditionality and Sanctions: A Report to the Secretary of State for Work and Pensions*. London. Available at https://www.gov.uk/government/publications/conditionality-and-sanctions-a-report-to-the-secretary-of-state-for-work-and-pensions.

Cowan, D., & Halliday, S. (2003). *The Appeal of Internal Review: Law, Administrative Justice, and the (Non-)Emergence of Disputes*. Oxford and Portland, OR: Hart Publishing.

Cowburn, A. (2017, February 5). Labour has Set Up a 'Working Group' to Investigate the Radical Idea of a Basic Income and will Report Back on its Conclusions before the next General Election, John McDonnell has said. *The Independent*.

Crowson, N. (2012). Revisiting the 1977 Housing (Homeless Persons) Act: Westminster, Whitehall and the Homelessness Lobby. *Twentieth Century British History, 24*(3), 424–447.

Deacon, A. (2000). Learning from the US? The Influence of American Ideas Upon 'New Labour' Thinking on Welfare Reform. *Policy and Politics, 28*(1), 5–18.

Department for Work and Pensions. (2013, September 10). *Jobseeker's Allowance: Overview of Revised Sanctions Regime.* Available at https://www.gov.uk/government/uploads/system/uploads/attachment_data/file/238839/jsa-overview-of-revised-sanctions-regime.pdf.

Department for Work and Pensions. (2014). *Fraud and Error in the Benefit System: 2012/13 Estimates (Great Britain).* Available at https://assets.publishing.service.gov.uk/government/uploads/system/uploads/attachment_data/file/271654/fraudand-error-in-the-benefit-system-2012-13_estimates-160114.pdf.

Department for Work and Pensions. (2016). *DWP Claimant Service and Experience Survey 2014/15.* London. Available at https://www.gov.uk/government/uploads/system/uploads/attachment_data/file/498207/rr916-dwp-claimant-service-and-experience-survey.pdf.

Department for Work and Pensions. (2018). *Guidance: Universal Credit.* London: GOV.UK. Available at https://www.gov.uk/government/publications/universal-credit-and-you/universal-credit-and-you-a.

Department of Social Security. (1998). *New Ambitions for Our Country: New Contract for Welfare,* Cm. 3805. London: HMSO.

Dicey, A. V. (1885/1979). *Introduction to the Study of the Law of the Constitution.* London: Palgrave Macmillan.

Dworkin, R. M. (1997). *Freedom's Law: The Moral Reading of the American Constitution.* Cambridge, MA: Harvard University Press.

Dwyer, P., & Wright, S. (2014). Universal Credit, Ubiquitous Conditionality and Its Implications for Social Citizenship. *Journal of Poverty and Social Justice, 22*(1), 27–35.

Dwyer, P., Jones, K., McNeill, J., Scullion, L., & Stewart, A. (2016). *First Wave Findings: Disability and Conditionality.* Available at http://www.welfareconditionality.ac.uk/wp-content/uploads/2016/05/WelCond-findings-disability-May16.pdf.

Eleveld, A. (2016). *Work-Related Sanctions in European Welfare States: An Incentive to Work or a Violation of Minimum Subsistence Rights?* (SSRN Research Paper 2016/01). Amsterdam: The Amsterdam Centre for Contemporary European Studies. Available at https://papers.ssrn.com/sol3/papers.cfm?abstract_id=2802656.

Esping-Andersen, G. (1990). *The Three Worlds of Welfare Capitalism.* Cambridge: Polity Press.

Etzioni, A. (1995). *The Spirit of Community.* London: Fontana.

Fitzpatrick, S., Bramley, G., Sosenko, F., Blenkinsopp, J., Johnsen, S., Littlewood, M., Netto, G., & Watts, B. (2016). *Destitution in the UK.* York: Joseph Rowntree Foundation. Available at https://www.jrf.org.uk/report/destitution-uk.

Flint, J. (2018). Encounters with the Centaur State: Advanced Urban Marginality and the Practices and Ethics if Welfare Sanctions Regimes. *Urban Studies.* Available online at https://www.urbanstudiesonline.com/mediacentre/news/encounters-with-the-centaur-state.

Foucault, M. (1979). *Discipline and Punish: The Birth of the Prison* (A. Sheridan, Trans.). New York: Vintage Books.

Fulbrook, J. (1978). *Administrative Justice and the Unemployed*. London: Mansell.

Gallie, W. B. (1955–1956). Essentially Contested Concepts. *Proceedings of the Aristotelian Society, 56*, 167–198. Reprinted as Chapter 8 in Gallie, W. B. (1964). *Philosophy and the Historical Understanding*. London: Chatto and Windus.

Garland, D. (2001). *The Culture of Control: Crime and the Social Order in Contemporary Society*. Oxford: Oxford University Press.

Genn, H. (2010). *Judging Civil Justice*. Cambridge: Cambridge University Press.

Giddens, A. (1984). *The Constitution of Society*. Cambridge: Polity Press.

Giddens, A. (1998). *The Third Way*. Cambridge: Polity Press.

Gregg, P. (2008). *Realising Potential: A Vision for Personalised Conditionality and Support (The Gregg Review)*. An independent report for the Department of Work and Pensions. Norwich: The Stationary Office. Available at http://www.dwp.gov.uk/docs/realisingpotential.pdf.

Griggs, J., & Evans, M. (2010). *Sanctions Within Conditional Benefit Systems: A Review of Evidence*. York: Joseph Rowntree Foundantion.

Grover, C. (2005). Advertising Social Security Fraud. *Benefits, 13*(3), 199–205.

Gulland, J. (2011). Ticking Boxes: Understanding Decision Making in Employment and Support Allowance. *Journal of Social Security Law, 18*(2), 69–86.

Gulland, J. (2017). Working While Incapable to Work? Changing Concepts of Permitted Work in the UK Disability Benefit System. *Disability Studies Quarterly, 37*(4). Available at https://doi.org/http://dx.doi.org/10.18061/dsq.v37i4.6088.

Hacker, J. S. (2002). *The Divided Welfare State: The Battle Over Public and Private Social Benefits in the United States*. Cambridge: Cambridge University Press.

Halliday, S. (2003). *Judicial Review and Compliance with Administrative Law*. Oxford: Hart Publishing.

Harris, N. (2010). Reducing Dependency? Conditional Rights, Benefit Reform and Drugs. *Journal of Law and Society, 37*(2), 233–262.

Hart, H. L. A. (1961/1972). *The Concept of Law*. Oxford: Oxford University Press.

Hayek, F. A. (1944). *The Road to Serfdom*. London: Routledge.

Hegarty, P. (2015, February 4). Work Programme Staff Were Told to Sanctions Against Clients. *New Statesman*.

Henman, P., & Fenger, M. (2006). Reforming Welfare Governance: Reflections. In P. Henman & M. Fenger (Eds.), *Administering Welfare Reform: International Transformations in Welfare Governance* (pp. 257–278). Bristol: Policy Press.

Hodge, M. (2016). *Called to Account*. London: Abacus.

House of Commons Public Accounts Committee. (2017, February 21). *Benefit Sanctions*, HC 775, 42nd Report of Session 2016–2017. Available at https://publications.parliament.uk/pa/cm201617/cmselect/cmpubacc/775/775.pdf.

House of Commons Work and Pensions Committee. (2015, March 24). *Benefit Sanctions Policy Beyond the Oakley Review*, HC 214, 5th Report of Session 2014–2015. Available at https://publications.parliament.uk/pa/cm201415/cmselect/cmworpen/814/814.pdf.

Jesse, J. T., & Tufte, P. A. (2007). Discretionary Decision-Making in a Changing Context of Activation Policies and Welfare Reforms. *Journal of Social Policy, 43*(2), 269–288.

Jobcentre Plus. (2011, March 9). *Parliamentary Briefing: Second Reading*. Available at https://fullfact.org/files/2011/03/Welfare_Reform_Bill_2R_Briefing.pdf.

Jones, E. (2016, May 23). Ken Loach Takes on Welfare System in I, Daniel Blake. *BBC News*.

Kelly, T. (2012). *This Side of Silence*. Philadelphia, PA: University of Pennsylvania Press.

King, D. S. (1987). *The New Right: Politics, Markets and Citizenship*. Basingstoke: Macmillan Education.

Knotz, C., & Nelson. M. (2013, September 5–7). *Quantifying Conditionality: A New Database on Conditions and Sanctions for Unemployment Benefit Claimants*. Paper prepared for the ESPAnet Conference, Poznan. Available at https://ssrn.com/abstract=2328253 or http://dx.doi.org/10.2189/ssrn.2328253.

Labour Party. (2017). *Election Manifesto: Social Security*. Available at https://labour.org.uk/manifesto/social-security/.

Landsbergen, D. (2004). Screen Level Bureaucracy: Databases as Public Records. *Government Information Quarterly, 21,* 25–50.

Langenbucher, K. (2015). *How Demanding are Eligibility Criteria for Unemployment Benefits—Quantitative Indicators for OECD and EU Countries* (OECD Social, Employment and Migration Papers, No. 166).

Larkin, P. (2007). The Criminalisation of Social Security Law: Towards a Punitive Welfare State. *Journal of Law and Society, 34*(3), 293–320.

Larkin, P. (2013). A Permanent Blow to Workfare in the United Kingdom or a Temporary Obstacle? Reilly and Wilson v Secretary of State for Work and Pensions. *Journal of Social Security Law, 20*(3), 110–118.

Larkin, P. (2015). Engaging with the Human Rights Angle: Reilly (No. 2) v Secretary of State for Work and Pensions. *Journal of Social Security Law, 22*(2), 85–94.

Lipsky, M. (1980). *Street-Level Bureaucracy: Dilemmas of the Individual in Public Services*. New York: Russell Sage Foundation.

Locke, J. (1689/1988). *Two Treatises of Government*. Cambridge Texts in the History of Political Thought. Cambridge: Cambridge University Press.

Loopstra, R., Reeves, A., McKee, M., & Suckler, D. (2015). *Do Punitive Approaches to Unemployment Benefit Recipients Increase Welfare Exit and Unemployment: A Cross-Area Analysis of UK Sanctioning Reforms* (Sociology Working Paper 2015-01), Department of Sociology, University of Oxford.

Available at http://www.sociology.ox.ac.uk/working-papers/do-punitive-approaches-to-unemployment-benefit-recipients-increase-welfare-exit-and-employment-a-cross-area-analysis-of-uk-sanctioning-reforms.html.

MacCormick, N. (2005). *Rhetoric and the Rule of Law: A Theory of Legal Reasoning*. Oxford: Oxford University Press.

Malik, S. (2015, August 5). Benefit sanctions: How estimated annual rates help scrutinise policy. *The Guardian*. Available at https://www.theguardian.com/politics/datablog/2015/aug/05/benefit-sanctions-estimated-annual-rates-scrutinise-dwp-policy.

Mann, M. (1987). Ruling Class Strategies and Citizenship. *Sociology, 21*(3), 339–354.

Marshall, T. H. (1963). Citizenship and Social Class. In *Sociology at the Crossroads* (Chapter 4). London: Routledge.

Mashaw, J. L. (1983). *Bureaucratic Justice: Managing Social Security*. New Haven and London: Yale University Press.

Mashaw, J. L. (1985). *Due Process in the Administrative State*. New Haven, CT: Yale University Press.

Millar, J. (2003). From Wage Replacement to Wage Supplement: Benefits and Tax Credits. In J. Millar (Ed.), *Understanding Social Security: Issues for Policy and Practice* (1st ed., pp. 123–143). Bristol: Policy Press.

Ministry of Justice. (2013). *Story of the Prison Population 1993–2012*. London: England and Wales.

Molander, A. (2016). *Discretion in the Welfare State*. London and New York: Routledge.

Molander, A., & Torsvik, G. (2015). Getting People into Work: What, (if Anything) Can Justify Mandatory Activation of Welfare Recipients? *Journal of Applied Philosophy, 32*(4), 373–392.

National Audit Office. (2016, November 17). *Benefit Sanctions: Detailed Methodology*. London: National Audit Office. Available at https://www.nao.org.uk/wp-content/uploads/2016/11/Benefit-sanctions-detailed-methodology.pdf.

Noyce, H. (2016, June 30). *UK Human Rights Blog*. Available at https://ukhumanrightsblog.com/2016/06/30/un-committee-seriously-concerned-about-the-impact-of-austerity-on-human-rights.

O'Malley, P. (2009). Theorizing Fines. *Punishment and Society, 11*(1), 67–83.

Oakley, M. (2014). *Independent Review of the Operation of Jobseeker's Allowance Sanctions Validated by the Jobseekers Act 2013*. London: Department of Work and Pensions. Available at https://www.gov.uk/government/uploads/system/uploads/attachment_data/file/335144/jsa-sanctions-independent-review.pdf.

OECD. (1984). *Tax Expenditures: A Review of the Issues and Country Practices*. Paris: OECD.

Piachaud, D. (2016, November). *Citizen's Income: Rights and Wrongs* (CASE/200). Centre for Analysis of Social Exclusion, London School of Economics.

Raz, J. (1979). The Rule of Law and Its Virtues. In *The Authority of Law: Essays on Law and Morality*. Oxford: Oxford University Press.

Richardson, G. (1984). The Legal Regulation of Process. In G. Richardson & H. Genn (Eds.), *Administrative Law and Government Action* (pp. 105–130). Oxford: Clarendon Press.

Royal Commission on the Taxation of Profits and Incomes (RCTPI). (1955). *Final Report*, Cmnd. 9474. London: HMSO.

Ryan, W. (1971). *Blaming the Victim*. New York: Pantheon Books.

Sainsbury, R. (2003). Understanding Social Security Fraud. In J. Millar (Ed.), *Understanding Social Security: Issues for Policy and Practice* (1st ed.). Bristol: The Policy Press.

Sainsbury, R. (2008). Administrative Justice, Discretion and the 'Welfare to Work' Project. *Journal of Social Welfare and Family Law, 30*(4), 323–338.

Sainsbury, R. (2009). Sickness, Incapacity and Disability. In J. Millar (Ed.), *Understanding Social Security: Issues for Policy and Practice* (2nd ed., pp. 213–232). Bristol: The Policy Press.

Scottish Government. (2012). *Prison Statistics and Population Projections 2001–2012*. Edinburgh.

Scottish Unemployed Workers' Network. (2014, December). *Sanctioned Voices: A Report on the Impact of the DWP Sanctions Regime as Implemented in Dundee Job Centre, Compiled by Volunteers for the Scottish Unemployed Workers' Network*. Available at https://suwn.files.wordpress.com/2015/12/sanctioned_voices.pdf.

Simpson, M. (2017). Renegotiating Social Citizenship in the Age of Devolution. *Journal of Law and Society, 44*(4), 646–673.

Simpson, M. (2018, forthcoming). Assessing the Compliance of the UK Social Security System with the State's Obligations under the European Social Charter. *European Human Rights Law Review*.

Sinfield, A. (1978). Analyses in the Social Division of Welfare. *Journal of Social Policy, 7*(2), 129–156.

Sinfield, A. (2001). Benefits and Research in the Labour Market. *European Journal of Social Security, 3*(3), 209–235.

Stone, J. (2015, November 12). Benefit Sanctions Against People with Mental Health Problems up by 600 Per Cent. *The Independent*. Available at http://www.independent.co.uk/news/uk/politics/benefit-sanctions-against-people-with-mental-health-problems-up-by-600-per-cent-a6731971.html.

Sykes, G. (1958/2007). *The Society of Captives: A Study of a Maximum-Security Prison*. Princeton, NJ: Princeton University Press.

Thomas, R. (2016). *The New Administrative Review: Administrative Justice in a Cold Climate*. Unpublished Paper.

Thomas, R., & Tomlinson, J. (2017). Mapping Current Issues in Administrative Justice: Austerity and the 'More Bureaucratic Rationality' Approach. *Journal of Social Welfare and Family Law, 39*(3), 380–399.

Timmins, N. (2016). *Universal Credit: From Disaster to Recovery?* London: Institute for Government.

Titmuss, R. (1965). *Essays on 'the Welfare State'* (2nd ed., pp. 34–55). London: Allen and Unwin.

Venn, D. (2012). *Eligibility Criteria or Unemployment Benefits—Quantitative Indicators for OECD and EU Countries* (OECD Social, Employment and Migration Papers, No. 131).

von Hirsch, A., & Ashworth, A. (2005). *Proportionate Sentencing.* Oxford: Oxford University Press, especially Chapter 9 entitled 'Criteria for Proportionality: A Review'.

Wacquant, L. (2009). *Punishing the Poor: The Neoliberal Government of Social Insecurity.* Durham, NC and London: Duke University Press.

Waldron, J. (2005). Is the Rule of Law an Essentially Contested Concept? In R. Bellamy (Ed.), *The Rule of Law and the Separation of Powers.* Farnham: Ashgate.

Waldron, J. (2008). *Cruel, Inhuman, and Degrading Treatment: The Words Themselves* (New York University Public Law and Legal Theory Working Papers, No. 98). Available at http://lsr.nellco.org/nyu_plltwp/98.

Walker, N. (1968). *Crime and Punishment in Britain.* Edinburgh: Edinburgh University Press.

Warren, N. (2006). The Adjudication Gap: A Discussion Document. *Journal of Social Security Law, 13*(2), 110–118.

Watts, B., Fitzpatrick, S., Bramley, G., & Watkins, D. (2014). *Welfare Sanctions and Conditionality in the UK.* York: Joseph Rowntree Foundation.

Webster, D. (2014, November 12). *Briefing: The DWP's JSA/ESA Sanctions Statistics Release.* Available at http://www.cpag.org/david-webster.

Webster, D. (2015a, February 18). *Briefing: The DWP's JSA/ESA Sanctions Statistics Release.* Available at http://www.cpag.org/david-webster.

Webster, D. (2015b, May 13). *Briefing: The DWP's JSA/ESA Sanctions Statistics Release.* Available at http://www.cpag.org/david-webster.

Webster, D. (2015c, November 18). *DWP Ad Hoc Statistical Release, JSA and ESA Hardship Applications and Awards: April 2012 to Jun 2015.* Available at http://www.cpag.org.uk/david-webster.

Webster, D. (2016a, May 18). *Briefing: The DWP's JSA/ESA Sanctions Statistics Release.* Available at http://www.cpag.org/david-webster.

Webster, D. (2016b, October 3). *Supplement: Explaining the rise and fall of JSA and ESA sanctions 2010-16.* Available at http://www.cpag.org/david-webster.

Webster, D. (2017a, February 22). *Briefing: The DWP's JSA/ESA Sanctions Statistics Release.* Available at http://www.cpag.org/david-webster.

Webster, D. (2017b, May 31). *Briefing: Benefit Sanctions Statistics: JSA, ESA, Universal Credit and Income Support for Lone Parents.* London: Child Poverty Action Group. Available at http://cpag.org.uk/david-webster.

White, S. (2017). Should a Minimum Income Be Unconditional? In S. C. Matteucci & S. Halliday (Eds.), *Social Rights in Europe in an Age of Austerity* (pp. 181–196). London and New York: Routledge.

Wintour, P. (2013, May 15). DWP Report Accepts Mistakes Made on Welfare Sanctions by Job Centres. *The Guardian*. Available at https://www.theguardian.com/society/2013/may/15/dwp-no-evidence-JobCentre-benefits-targets.

Wolffe, W. J. (2014, December). *Economic and Social Rights in Scotland: Lessons from the Past: Options for the Future.* A Lecture for International Human Rights Day 2014. Edinburgh Law School. Available at http://www.scottishhumanrights.com/media/1469/wolffe2014lecture.pdf.

Wright, S. (2003). The Street-Level Implementation of Unemployment Policy. In J. Millar (Ed.), *Understanding Social Security: Issues for policy and Practice* (1st ed., pp. 235–253). Bristol: Policy Press.

Wright, S. (2006). The Administration of Transformation: A Case Study of Implementing Welfare Reform in the UK. In P. Henman & M. Fenger (Eds.), *Administering Welfare Reform: International Transformations in Welfare Governance* (pp. 161–182). Bristol: Policy Press.

Wright, S. (2009). Welfare to Work. In J. Millar (Ed.), *Understanding Social Security: Issues for policy and Practice* (2nd ed., pp. 193–202). Bristol: Policy Press.

Wright, S., & Stewart, A. (2016). *First Wave Findings: Jobseekers.* Available at http://www.welfareconditionality.ac.uk/wp-content/uploads/2016/05/WelCond-findings-jobseekers-May16.pdf.

# Author Index

© The Editor(s) (if applicable) and The Author(s) 2018
M. Adler, *Cruel, Inhuman or Degrading Treatment?*, Palgrave
Socio-Legal Studies, https://doi.org/10.1007/978-3-319-90356-9

# Subject Index

**A**

activation, 28, 29, 33, 34, 65, 66, 91, 144

adjudication, 91, 92, 100, 101, 111, 119, 126, 132, 134

adjudication officers, 22, 92

administrative justice, 5, 6, 9, 33, 87–96, 99–103, 107

  bureaucratic model, 90, 92, 93, 95, 100

  consumerist model, 90, 102

  effect of organisational changes on, 87, 91

  juridical model, 90, 92, 100, 107

  managerial model, 90

  market model, 90, 95, 101

  need for empirical research on, 102

  normative models, 87, 89–91

  professional model, 90, 93, 100

  trade-offs, 87, 90, 103

**B**

basic income, 138, 144

benefit fraud, 17, 29

benefit sanctions, 4–6, 9, 11–14, 18, 19, 21–23, 29, 36, 37, 40, 42, 45–47, 50, 54, 57, 60, 63, 64, 71, 73, 74, 77, 78, 82, 84, 87, 91, 92, 96, 97, 99, 102, 103, 107, 108, 111, 113, 115–127, 129, 131, 132, 134, 135, 137–141, 143–145, 149–151

  current regime, 4, 22, 150, 151

  explaining rise and fall, 45, 48, 50

  incidence, 46, 60, 118, 119

  scope, 6, 37, 40, 42, 45, 46, 60, 143

  severity, 6, 42, 45, 46, 60, 119, 143

Beveridge Report, 24, 25

blaming the victim, 13

British Social Attitudes Survey, 14

  Survey of attitudes to government spending on claimants, 40

  Survey of deservingness of benefit claimants, 14

  Survey of perceived standards of living of unemployed, 6

© The Editor(s) (if applicable) and The Author(s) 2018
M. Adler, *Cruel, Inhuman or Degrading Treatment?*, Palgrave
Socio-Legal Studies, https://doi.org/10.1007/978-3-319-90356-9